Johann Ludwig Uhland

Selections from Ballads and Romances

Johann Ludwig Uhland

Selections from Ballads and Romances

ISBN/EAN: 9783744664905

Hergestellt in Europa, USA, Kanada, Australien, Japan

Cover: Foto ©Thomas Meinert / pixelio.de

Weitere Bücher finden Sie auf **www.hansebooks.com**

SELECTIONS

FROM

UHLAND'S BALLADS AND ROMANCES

WITH BIOGRAPHICAL NOTICES, AND HISTORICAL

AND GRAMMATICAL NOTES

BY

G. EUGÈNE FASNACHT

London

MACMILLAN AND CO.

AND NEW YORK

1888

First Edition printed 1882.
Reprinted 1888.

PREFACE.

THE remarkable simplicity of Uhland's poetry, simple not only in language and style but also in thought and sentiment, marks out his poems from among all German literature as eminently fitted for the study of young beginners. No easier, and at the same time no more captivating, readings can possibly—I speak from long experience—be placed in the hands of English boys and girls.

Some of his best romances, as "Bertrand de Born," "Der Waller," "Das Schlosz am Meer," and a few others, will no doubt be missed by old friends of the poet; but as the selection has been made especially with a view to suit the capacities of mere tyros in the language, I had no alternative but to exclude all poems, however excellent, which either in thought or in language seemed to me to be beyond the grasp of those for whom the selection is intended.

BIOGRAPHICAL NOTICE.

JOHANN LUDWIG UHLAND was born at Tubingen, in the kingdom of Würtemberg, on the 26th of April 1787. He early devoted himself to the study of law in the university of his native town, but felt himself more powerfully attracted towards the cultivation of the Muses. His first poems date from his fourteenth year. Having matriculated, and in due course taken his degree of Doctor of Laws (1810), he availed himself of a stipend to pursue his law studies in Paris, especially with a view to make himself acquainted with the *Code Napoleon*. In reality, however, he spent the best of his time in deciphering in the Imperial library the manuscripts of mediæval French literature. It is to this period of his life that we are indebted for some of his best ballads, particularly those bearing upon the ancient troubadours and trouvères (Durand, der Castellan von Coucy, Taillefer, etc.)

Though we are only concerned here with Uhland the poet, it would be doing but scant justice to his character if we were not to mention, though only incidentally, his almost lifelong struggles in the cause of the constitutional freedom of his native country.

Elected a member of the Würtembergian Parliament (Stände-Versammlung) for the electoral district of Tubingen (1819), he proved himself throughout his long parliamentary career one of the staunchest supporters of the old time-honoured Charter (Das gute alte Recht) which King William attempted to suppress. In this period fall his political poems, which, at the outset, won for him great popularity, and contributed to awaken his fellow-countrymen to a sense of their civic duties.

No less distinguished were his labours in the field of scholarship. His essay on "Old French Epic Poetry" (1812), on "Walther von der Vogelweide" (1822), his excellent collection of Popular Songs (1844-5), and a few other writings, subsequently collected and published under the title of *Uhland's Schriften zur Geschichte der Dichtung und Sage* (1865), claim for him a very high rank among

German scholars. His contributions to dramatic literature, however, "Herzog Ernst von Schwaben" (1817), and "Ludwig der Baier" (1819), although noble conceptions, are wanting in dramatic life, and cannot be said to have added to his fame as a poet.

In 1830 he was appointed Professor of the German Language and Literature at the University of Tubingen, but he soon resigned this post when he found it incompatible with his parliamentary duties. He died after a protracted illness on the 13th of November 1862.

We conclude with an article on "Uhland" in the English Cyclopædia, in which the characteristic features of his poetry are well appreciated:—

"His songs, ballads, and romances form the most valuable portion of Uhland's literary works. His songs are distinguished by their spirit and energy, their truth and depth of feeling, their lively and picturesque representations of nature, and their varied subjects; his patriotic songs, in particular, contain some heart-stirring appeals to all the better national feelings that were likely to arouse his countrymen, and in them is a mixture of earnestness and jocularity, with a fervent love of country, and aspiration after the great and good inspired by the recollections of their ancestors. His ballads and romances are remarkable for their apparent simplicity, the result of a most carefully exercised art, shown by the extreme skill and felicity in the choice of words, and the masterly way in which characters are sketched perfectly but briefly."

CONTENTS.

		PAGE
BIOGRAPHICAL NOTICE	. . . .	vii
I. DER WEISZE HIRSCH (1811)	. . .	1
II. DIE EINKEHR (1811)	. . . .	2
III. DIE RACHE (1810)	. . . .	2
IV. DAS SCHWERT (1809)	. . . .	3
V. SIEGFRIED'S SCHWERT (1812)	. . .	3
VI. DER GUTE KAMERAD (1809)	. . .	4
VII. DES KNABEN BERGLIED (1806)	. . .	5
VIII. SCHWÄBISCHE KUNDE (1814)	. . .	6
IX. KLEIN ROLAND (1808)	. . . .	7
X. ROLAND SCHILDTRÄGER (1811)	. . .	12
XI. KÖNIG KARL'S MEERFAHRT (1812)	. .	18
XII. TAILLEFER (1811)	. . . . .	20
XIII. DAS GLÜCK VON EDENHALL (1834)	. .	22
XIV. DES SÄNGERS FLUCH (1814)	. . .	24
XV. DER BLINDE KÖNIG (1804)	. . . .	26
NOTES	. . . . . .	29

I. Der weiße Hirsch.

Es gingen drei Jäger wol auf die Birsch,
Sie wollten erjagen den weißen Hirsch.

Sie legten sich unter den Tannenbaum,
Da hatten die Drei einen seltsamen Traum.

Der Erste.

"Mir hat geträumt, ich klopf' auf den Busch,
Da rauschte der Hirsch heraus, husch husch!"

Der Zweite.

"Und als er sprang mit der Hunde Geklaff,
Da brannt' ich ihm auf das Fell, piff paff!"

Der Dritte.

"Und als ich den Hirsch auf der Erde sah,
Da stieß ich lustig ins Horn, trara!"

So lagen sie da und sprachen, die Drei,
Da rannte der weiße Hirsch vorbei.

Und eh' die Jäger ihn recht gesehn,
So war er davon über Tiefen und Höhn.
Husch husch! Piff paff! Trara!

II. Einkehr.

Bei einem Wirte, wundermild,
Da war ich jüngst zu Gaste;
Ein goldner Apfel war sein Schild
An einem langen Aste.

Es war der gute Apfelbaum,
Bei dem ich eingekehret;
Mit süßer Kost und frischem Schaum
Hat er mich wol genähret.

Es kamen in sein grünes Haus
Viel leichtbeschwingte Gäste;
Sie sprangen frei und hielten Schmaus
Und sangen auf das beste.

Ich fand ein Bett zu süßer Ruh
Auf weichen grünen Matten;
Der Wirt, er deckte selbst mich zu
Mit seinem kühlen Schatten.

Nun fragt' ich nach der Schuldigkeit,
Da schüttelt' er den Wipfel.
Gesegnet sei er allezeit
Von der Wurzel bis zum Gipfel!

III. Die Rache.

Der Knecht hat erstochen den edeln Herrn,
Der Knecht wär' selber ein Ritter gern.

Er hat ihn erstochen im dunkeln Hain
Und den Leib versenket im tiefen Rhein;

Hat angelegt die Rüstung blank,
Auf des Herren Roß sich geschwungen frank.

Und als er sprengen will über die Brück',
Da stutzet das Roß und bäumt sich zurück.

Und als er die güldnen Sporen ihm gab,
Da schleudert's ihn wild in den Strom hinab.　10

Mit Arm, mit Fuß er rudert und ringt,
Der schwere Panzer ihn niederzwingt.

IV. Das Schwert.

Zur Schmiede ging ein junger Held,
Er hatt' ein gutes Schwert bestellt.
Doch als er's wog in freier Hand,
Das Schwert er viel zu schwer erfand.

Der alte Schmied den Bart sich streicht:　5
„Das Schwert ist nicht zu schwer noch leicht,
Zu schwach ist Euer Arm, ich mein';
Doch morgen soll geholfen sein."

„Nein, heut', bei aller Ritterschaft!
Durch meine, nicht durch Feuers Kraft."　10
Der Jüngling spricht's, ihn Kraft durchdringt,
Das Schwert er hoch in Lüften schwingt.

V. Siegfried's Schwert.

Jung Siegfried war ein stolzer Knab',
Ging von des Vaters Burg herab.

Wollt' rasten nicht in Vaters Haus,
Wollt' wandern in alle Welt hinaus.

Begegnet' ihm manch Ritter wert　5
Mit festem Schild und breitem Schwert.

Siegfried nur einen Stecken trug,
Das war ihm bitter und leid genug.

Und als er ging im finstern Wald,
Kam er zu einer Schmiede bald.

Da sah er Eisen und Stahl genug,
Ein lustig Feuer Flammen schlug.

„O Meister, liebster Meister mein,
Laß du mich deinen Gesellen sein.

Und lehr' du mich mit Fleiß und Acht,
Wie man die guten Schwerter macht!"

Siegfried den Hammer wohl schwingen kunnt',
Er schlug den Amboß in den Grund.

Er schlug, daß weit der Wald erklang
Und alles Eisen in Stücke sprang.

Und von der letzten Eisenstang'
Macht' er ein Schwert, so breit und lang.

„Nun hab' ich geschmiedet ein gutes Schwert,
Nun bin ich wie andre Ritter wert;

Nun schlag' ich wie ein anderer Held
Die Riesen und Drachen in Wald und Feld."

VI. Der gute Kamerad.

Ich hatt' einen Kameraden,
Einen bessern find'st du nit.
Die Trommel schlug zum Streite,
Er ging an meiner Seite
In gleichem Schritt und Tritt.

Eine Kugel kam geflogen,
Gilt's mir oder gilt es dir?
Ihn hat es weggerissen,
Er liegt mir vor den Füßen,
Als wär's ein Stück von mir. 10

Will mir die Hand noch reichen,
Derweil ich eben lad'.
Kann dir die Hand nicht geben;
Bleib du im ew'gen Leben
Mein guter Kamerad! 15

VII. Des Knaben Berglied.

Ich bin vom Berg der Hirtenknab',
Seh' auf die Schlösser all' herab.
Die Sonne strahlt am ersten hier,
Am längsten weilet sie bei mir.
Ich bin der Knab' vom Berge. 5

Hier ist des Stromes Mutterhaus,
Ich trink' ihn frisch vom Stein heraus,
Er braust vom Fels in wildem Lauf,
Ich fang' ihn mit den Armen auf.
Ich bin der Knab' vom Berge. 10

Der Berg, der ist mein Eigentum,
Da ziehn die Stürme rings herum,
Und heulen sie von Nord und Süd,
So überschallt sie doch mein Lied:
„Ich bin der Knab' vom Berge." 15

Sind Blitz und Donner unter mir,
So steh' ich hoch im Blauen hier;
Ich kenne sie und rufe zu:
„Laßt meines Vaters Haus in Ruh'!
Ich bin der Knab' vom Berge!" 20

Und wenn die Sturmglock' einst erschallt,
Manch Feuer auf den Bergen wallt,
Dann steig' ich nieder, tret' ins Glied
Und schwing' mein Schwert und sing' mein Lied:
„Ich bin der Knab vom Berge!" 25

VIII. Schwäbische Kunde.

Als Kaiser Rotbart lobesam
Zum heil'gen Land gezogen kam,
Da mußt' er mit dem frommen Heer
Durch ein Gebirge, wüst und leer.
Daselbst erhub sich große Not, 5
Viel Steine gab's und wenig Brot,
Und mancher deutsche Reitersmann
Hat dort den Trunk sich abgethan.
Den Pferden war's so schwach im Magen,
Fast mußt' der Reiter die Mähre tragen. 10
Nun war ein Herr aus Schwabenland
Von hohem Wuchs und starker Hand,
Des Rößlein war so krank und schwach,
Er zog es nur am Zaume nach;
Er hätt' es nimmer aufgegeben, 15
Und kostet's ihm das eigne Leben.
So blieb er bald ein gutes Stück
Hinter dem Heereszug zurück.
Da sprengten plötzlich in die Quer
Fünfzig türkische Reiter daher, 20
Die huben an, auf ihn zu schießen,
Nach ihm zu werfen mit den Spießen.
Der wackre Schwabe forcht sich nit,
Ging seines Weges Schritt vor Schritt,
Ließ sich den Schild mit Pfeilen spicken 25
Und thät nur spöttlich um sich blicken,
Bis Einer, dem die Zeit zu lang,

Auf ihn den krummen Säbel schwang.
Da wallt dem Deutschen auch sein Blut,
Er trifft des Türken Pferd so gut, 30
Er haut ihm ab mit einem Streich
Die beiden Vorderfüß' zugleich.
Als er das Tier zu Fall gebracht,
Da faßt er erst sein Schwert mit Macht,
Er schwingt es auf des Reiters Kopf, 35
Haut durch bis auf den Sattelknopf,
Haut auch den Sattel noch in Stücken
Und tief noch in des Pferdes Rücken.
Zur Rechten sieht man wie zur Linken
Einen halben Türken heruntersinken. 40
Da packt die Andern kalter Graus,
Sie fliehen in alle Welt hinaus,
Und Jedem ist's, als würd' ihm mitten
Durch Kopf und Leib hindurch geschnitten.
Drauf kam des Wegs 'ne Christenschaar, 45
Die auch zurückgeblieben war.
Die sahen nun mit gutem Bedacht,
Was Arbeit unser Held gemacht.
Von denen hat's der Kaiser vernommen;
Der ließ den Schwaben vor sich kommen; 50
Er sprach: „Sag an, mein Ritter wert!
Wer hat dich solche Streich' gelehrt?"
Der Held besann sich nicht zu lang':
„Die Streiche sind bei uns im Schwang,
Sie sind bekannt im ganzen Reiche, 55
Man nennt sie halt nur Schwabenstreiche."

IX.—Klein Roland.

Frau Bertha saß in der Felsenkluft,
Sie klagt' ihr bitteres Los.
Klein Roland spielt' in freier Luft,
Des Klage war nicht groß.

„O König Karl, mein Bruder hehr,
O daß ich floh von dir!
Um Liebe ließ ich Pracht und Ehr',
Nun zürnst du schrecklich mir.

O Milon, mein Gemahl so süß!
Die Flut verschlang mir dich.
Die ich um Liebe Alles ließ,
Nun läßt die Liebe mich.

Klein Roland, du mein teures Kind,
Nun Ehr' und Liebe mir!
Klein Roland, komm herein geschwind!
Mein Trost kommt all von dir.

Klein Roland, geh zur Stadt hinab,
Zu bitten um Speis' und Trank,
Und wer dir giebt eine kleine Gab',
Dem wünsche Gottes Dank!"

Der König Karl zur Tafel saß
Im goldnen Rittersaal.
Die Diener liefen ohn' Unterlaß
Mit Schüssel und Pokal.

Von Flöten, Saitenspiel, Gesang
Ward jedes Herz erfreut,
Doch reichte nicht der helle Klang
Zu Berthas Einsamkeit.

Und draußen in des Hofes Kreis,
Da saßen der Bettler viel,
Die labten sich an Trank und Speis'
Mehr als am Saitenspiel.

Der König schaut in ihr Gedräng'
Wohl durch die offne Thür,
Da drückt sich durch die dichte Meng
Ein feiner Knab' herfür.

Des Knaben Kleid ist wunderbar,
Vierfarb zusammengestückt;
Doch weilt er nicht bei der Bettlerschar,
Herauf zum Saal er blickt.   40

Herein zum Saal klein Roland tritt,
Als wär's sein eigen Haus.
Er hebt eine Schüssel von Tisches Mitt'
Und trägt sie stumm hinaus.

Der König denkt: was muß ich sehn?   45
Das ist ein sondrer Brauch.
Doch weil er's ruhig läßt geschehn,
So lassen's die Andern auch.

Es stund nur an eine kleine Weil',
Klein Roland kehrt in den Saal.   50
Er tritt zum König hin mit Eil'
Und faßt seinen Goldpokal.

„Heida! Halt an, du kecker Wicht!"
Der König ruft es laut.
Klein Roland läßt den Becher nicht,   55
Zum König auf er schaut.

Der König erst gar finster sah,
Doch lachen mußt' er bald.
„Du trittst in die goldne Halle da
Wie in den grünen Wald.   60

Du nimmst die Schüssel von Königs Tisch,
Wie man Aepfel bricht vom Baum;
Du holst wie aus dem Brunnen frisch
Meines roten Weines Schaum."

„Die Bäurin schöpft aus dem Brunnen frisch   65
Die bricht die Aepfel vom Baum;
Meiner Mutter ziemet Wildbret und Fisch,
Ihr roten Weines Schaum." —

„Ist deine Mutter so edle Dam',
Wie du berühmst, mein Kind,
So hat sie wohl ein Schloß lustsam
Und stattlich Hofgesind'?

Sag an: wer ist denn ihr Truchseß?
Sag' an: wer ist ihr Schenk?" —
„Meine rechte Hand ist ihr Truchseß,
Meine linke, die ist ihr Schenk." —

„Sag' an: wer sind die Wächter treu?"
„Mein' Augen blau allstund." —
„Sag' an: wer ist ihr Sänger frei?" —
„Der ist mein roter Mund." —

„Die Dam' hat wackre Diener, traun!
Doch liebt sie sondre Livrei,
Wie Regenbogen anzuschaun
Mit Farben mancherlei!" —

„Ich hab' bezwungen der Knaben acht
Von jedem Viertel der Stadt,
Die haben mir als Zins gebracht
Vierfältig Tuch zur Wat." —

„Die Dame hat nach meinem Sinn
Den besten Diener der Welt.
Sie ist wohl Bettlerkönigin,
Die offne Tafel hält?

So edle Dame darf nicht fern
Von meinem Hofe sein.
Wohlauf, drei Damen! Auf, drei Herrn!
Führt sie zu mir herein!"

Klein Roland trägt den Becher flink
Hinaus zum Prunkgemach;
Drei Damen auf des Königs Wink,
Drei Ritter folgen nach.

Es stund nur an eine kleine Weil',
Der König schaut in die Fern',
Da kehren schon zurück mit Eil'
Die Damen und die Herrn.

Der König ruft mit einem Mal: 105
„Hilf, Himmel! Seh' ich recht?
Ich hab' verspottet im offnen Saal
Mein eigenes Geschlecht.

Hilf, Himmel! Schwester Bertha, bleich,
Im grauen Pilgergewand! 110
Hilf, Himmel, in meinem Prunksaal reich
Den Bettelstab in der Hand!"

Frau Bertha fällt zu Füßen ihm,
Das bleiche Frauenbild.
Da regt sich plötzlich der alte Grimm, 115
Er blickt sie an so wild.

Frau Bertha senkt die Augen schnell,
Kein Wort zu reden sich traut.
Klein Roland hebt die Augen hell,
Den Ohm begrüßt er laut. 120

Da spricht der König mit mildem Ton:
„Steh auf, du Schwester mein!
Um diesen deinen lieben Sohn
Soll dir verziehen sein."

Frau Bertha hebt sich freudenvoll: 125
„Lieb Bruder mein, wohlan!
Klein Roland dir vergelten soll,
Was du mir Guts gethan.

Soll werden, seinem König gleich,
Ein hohes Heldenbild; 130
Soll führen die Farb' von manchem Reich
In seinem Banner und Schild.

Soll greifen in manches Königs Tisch
Mit seiner freien Hand;
Soll bringen zu Heil und Ehren frisch   135
Sein seufzend Mutterland."

X. Roland Schildträger.

Der König Karl saß einst zu Tisch
Zu Aachen mit den Fürsten;
Man stellte Wildbret auf und Fisch
Und ließ auch Keinen dürsten.
Viel Goldgeschirr von klarem Schein,   5
Manch rothen, grünen Edelstein
Sah man im Saale leuchten.

Da sprach Herr Karl, der starke Held:
„Was soll der eitle Schimmer?
Das beste Kleinod dieser Welt,   10
Das fehlet uns noch immer.
Dies Kleinod, hell wie Sonnenschein,
Ein Riese trägt's im Schilde sein
Tief im Ardennerwalde."

Graf Richard, Erzbischof Turpin,   15
Herr Haimon, Naims von Baiern,
Milon von Anglant, Graf Garin,
Die wollten da nicht feiern.
Sie haben Stahlgewand begehrt
Und hießen satteln ihre Pferd',   20
Zu reiten nach dem Riesen.

Jung Roland, Sohn des Milon, sprach:
„Lieb Vater, hört, ich bitte!
Vermeint Ihr mich zu jung und schwach,
Daß ich mit Riesen stritte,   25

Doch bin ich nicht zu winzig mehr,
Euch nachzutragen Euern Speer
Sammt Euerm guten Schilde."

Die sechs Genossen ritten bald
Vereint nach den Ardennen; 30
Doch als sie kamen in den Wald,
Da thäten sie sich trennen.
Roland ritt hinterm Vater her;
Wie wohl ihm war, des Helden Speer,
Des Helden Schild zu tragen! 35

Bei Sonnenschein und Mondenlicht
Streiften die kühnen Degen;
Doch fanden sie den Riesen nicht
In Felsen und Gehegen.
Zur Mittagsstund' am vierten Tag 40
Der Herzog Milon schlafen lag
In einer Eiche Schatten.

Roland sah in der Ferne bald
Ein Blitzen und ein Leuchten,
Davon die Strahlen in dem Wald 45
Die Hirsch' und Reh' aufscheuchten;
Er sah, es kam von einem Schild,
Den trug ein Riese, groß und wild,
Vom Berge niedersteigend.

Roland gedacht' im Herzen sein: 50
Was ist das für ein Schrecken!
Soll ich den lieben Vater mein
Im besten Schlaf erwecken?
Es wachet ja sein gutes Pferd,
Es wacht sein Speer, sein Schild und Schwert, 55
Es wacht Roland, der junge.

Roland das Schwert zur Seite band,
Herrn Milons starkes Waffen,

Die Lanze nahm er in die Hand.
Und thät den Schild aufraffen; 60
Herrn Milons Roß bestieg er dann
Und ritt erst sachte durch den Tann,
Den Vater nicht zu wecken.

Und als er kam zur Felsenwand,
Da sprach der Ries' mit Lachen: 65
„Was will doch dieser kleine Fant
Auf solchem Rosse machen?
Sein Schwert ist zwier so lang als er,
Vom Rosse zieht ihn schier der Speer,
Der Schild will ihn erdrücken." 70

Jung Roland rief: „Wohlauf zum Streit!
Dich reuet noch dein Necken.
Hab' ich die Tartsche lang und breit,
Kann sie mich besser decken;
Ein kleiner Mann, ein großes Pferd, 75
Ein kurzer Arm, ein langes Schwert,
Muß Eins dem Andern helfen."

Der Riese mit der Stange schlug,
Auslangend in die Weite;
Jung Roland schwenkte schnell genug 80
Sein Roß noch auf die Seite.
Die Lanz' er auf den Riesen schwang,
Doch von dem Wunderschilde sprang
Auf Roland sie zurücke.

Jung Roland nahm in großer Hast 85
Das Schwert in beide Hände;
Der Riese nach dem seinen faßt',
Er war zu unbehende;
Mit flinkem Hiebe schlug Roland
Ihm unterm Schild die linke Hand 90
Daß Hand und Schild entrollten.

Dem Riesen schwand der Mut dahin,
Wie ihm der Schild entrissen;
Das Kleinod, das ihm Kraft verliehn,
Mußt' er mit Schmerzen missen. 95
Zwar lief er gleich dem Schilde nach,
Doch Roland in das Knie ihn stach,
Daß er zu Boden stürzte.
Roland ihn bei den Haaren griff,
Hieb ihm das Haupt herunter; 100
Ein großer Strom von Blute lief
Ins tiefe Thal hinunter;
Und aus des Toten Schild hernach
Roland das lichte Kleinod brach
Und freute sich am Glanze. 105
Dann barg er's unterm Kleide gut
Und ging zu einem Quelle,
Da wusch er sich von Staub und Blut
Gewand und Waffen helle.
Zurücke ritt der jung' Roland 110
Dahin, wo er den Vater fand
Noch schlafend bei der Eiche.
Er legt' sich an des Vaters Seit',
Vom Schlafe selbst bezwungen,
Bis in der kühlen Abendzeit 115
Herr Milon aufgesprungen:
„Wach' auf, wach' auf, mein Sohn Roland!
Nimm Schild und Lanze schnell zur Hand,
Daß wir den Riesen suchen!"
Sie stiegen auf und eilten sehr, 120
Zu schweifen in der Wilde;
Roland ritt hinterm Vater her
Mit dessen Speer und Schilde.
Sie kamen bald zu jener Stätt',
Wo Roland jüngst gestritten hätt'; 125
Der Riese lag im Blute.

Roland kaum seinen Augen glaubt',
Als nicht mehr war zu schauen
Die linke Hand, dazu das Haupt,
So er ihm abgehauen, 130
Nicht mehr des Riesen Schwert und Speer,
Auch nicht sein Schild und Harnisch mehr,
Nur Rumpf und blut'ge Glieder.

Milon besah den großen Rumpf:
„Was ist das für 'ne Leiche? 135
Man sieht noch am zerhaunen Stumpf,
Wie mächtig war die Eiche.
Das ist der Riese! Frag' ich mehr?
Verschlafen hab' ich Sieg und Ehr',
Drum muß ich ewig trauern." 140

Zu Aachen vor dem Schlosse stund
Der König Karl gar bange:
„Sind meine Helden wohl gesund?
Sie weilen allzu lange.
Doch seh' ich recht, auf Königswort! 145
So reitet Herzog Haimon dort,
Des Riesen Haupt am Speere."

Herr Haimon ritt in trübem Muth,
Und mit gesenktem Spieße
Legt' er das Haupt, besprengt mit Blut, 150
Dem König vor die Füße:
„Ich fand den Kopf im wilden Hag,
Und fünfzig Schritte weiter lag
Des Riesen Rumpf am Boden."

Bald auch der Erzbischof Turpin 155
Den Riesenhandschuh brachte,
Die ungefüge Hand noch drin;
Er zog sie aus und lachte:
„Das ist ein schön Reliquienstück,

Ich bring' es aus dem Wald zurück, 160
Fand es schon zugehauen."

Der Herzog Naims von Baierland
Kam mit des Riesen Stange:
„Schaut an, was ich im Walde fand!
Ein Waffen, stark und lange. 165
Wohl schwitz' ich von dem schweren Druck;
Hei! Bairisch Bier, ein guter Schluck,
Sollt' mir gar köstlich munden!"

Graf Richard kam zu Fuß daher,
Ging neben seinem Pferde; 170
Das trug des Riesen schwere Wehr,
Den Harnisch sammt dem Schwerte:
„Wer suchen will im wilden Tann,
Manch Waffenstück noch finden kann,
Ist mir zu viel gewesen." 175

Der Graf Garin thät ferne schon
Den Schild des Riesen schwingen.
„Der hat den Schild, des ist die Kron',
Der wird das Kleinod bringen!" —
„Den Schild hab' ich, ihr lieben Herrn; 180
Das Kleinod hätt' ich gar zu gern,
Doch das ist ausgebrochen."

Zuletzt thät man Herrn Milon sehn,
Der nach dem Schlosse lenkte;
Er ließ das Rößlein langsam gehn, 185
Das Haupt er traurig senkte.
Roland ritt hinterm Vater her
Und trug ihm seinen starken Speer
Zusammt dem festen Schilde.

Doch wie sie kamen vor das Schloß 190
Und zu den Herrn geritten,
Macht' er von Vaters Schilde los

Den Zierat in der Mitten;
Das Riesenkleinod setzt' er ein,
Das gab so wunderklaren Schein 195
Als wie die liebe Sonne.

Und als nun diese helle Glut
Im Schilde Milons brannte,
Da rief der König wohlgemut:
„Heil Milon von Anglante! 200
Der hat den Riesen übermannt,
Ihm abgeschlagen Haupt und Hand,
Das Kleinod ihm entrissen."

Herr Milon hatte sich gewandt,
Sah staunend all die Helle: 205
„Roland, sag' an, du junger Fant,
Wer gab dir das, Geselle?"—
„Um Gott, Herr Vater, zürnt mir nicht,
Daß ich erschlug den groben Wicht,
Derweil Ihr eben schliefet!" 210

XI. König Karl's Meerfahrt.

Der König Karl fuhr über Meer
Mit seinen zwölf Genossen:
Zum heil'gen Lande steuert' er
Und ward vom Sturm verstoßen.

Da sprach der kühne Held Roland: 5
„Ich kann wol fechten und schirmen;
Doch hält mir diese Kunst nicht Stand
Vor Wellen und vor Stürmen."

Dann sprach Herr Holger aus Dänemark:
„Ich kann die Harfe schlagen; 10
Was hilft mir das, wenn also stark
Die Wind' und Wellen jagen?"

Herr Oliver war auch nicht froh,
Er sah auf seine Wehre:
„Es ist mir um mich selbst nicht so
Wie um die Altekläre."

Dann sprach der schlimme Ganelon,
Er sprach es nur verstohlen:
„Wär ich mit guter Art davon,
Möcht' euch der Teufel holen!"

Erzbischof Turpin seufzte sehr:
„Wir sind die Gottesstreiter;
Komm, liebster Heiland, über das Meer
Und führ' uns gnädig weiter!"

Graf Richard Ohnefurcht hub an:
„Ihr Geister aus der Hölle,
Ich hab euch manchen Dienst gethan,
Jetzt helft mir von der Stelle!"

Herr Naimis diesen Ausspruch that:
„Schon Vielen riet ich heuer,
Doch süßes Wasser und guter Rat
Sind oft zu Schiffe teuer."

Da sprach der graue Herr Riol:
„Ich bin ein alter Degen
Und möchte meinen Leichnam wohl
Dereinst ins Trockne legen."

Es war Herr Gui, ein Ritter fein,
Der fing wohl an zu singen:
„Ich wollt', ich wär' ein Vögelein,
Wollt' mich zu Liebchen schwingen."

Da sprach der edle Graf Garein:
„Gott helf' uns aus der Schwere!
Ich trink' viel lieber den roten Wein
Als Wasser in dem Meere."

Herr Lambert sprach, ein Jüngling frisch: 45
Gott woll' uns nicht vergessen!
Äß' lieber selbst 'nen guten Fisch,
Statt daß mich Fische fressen."

Da sprach Herr Gottfried lobesan:
„Ich laß mir's halt gefallen; 50
Man richtet mir nichts anders an
Als meinen Brüdern allen."

Der König Karl am Steuer saß,
Der hat kein Wort gesprochen,
Er lenkt das Schiff mit festem Maß, 55
Bis sich der Sturm gebrochen.

XII. Taillefer.

Normannenherzog Wilhelm sprach einmal:
„Wer singet in meinem Hof und in meinem Saal?
Wer singet vom Morgen bis in die späte Nacht
So lieblich, daß mir das Herz im Leibe lacht?"

„Das ist Taillefer, der so gerne singt, 5
Im Hofe, wenn er das Rad am Brunnen schwingt,
Im Saale, wenn er das Feuer schüret und facht,
Wenn er Abends sich legt, und wenn er Morgens erwacht."

Der Herzog sprach: „Ich hab' einen guten Knecht,
Den Taillefer, der dienet mir fromm und recht; 10
Er treibt mein Rad und schüret mein Feuer gut,
Und singet so hell, das höhet mir den Mut."

Da sprach der Taillefer: „Und wär' ich frei,
Viel besser wollt' ich dienen und singen dabei.
Wie wollt' ich dienen dem Herzog hoch zu Pferd! 15
Wie wollt' ich singen und klingen mit Schild und mit Schwert!"

Nicht lange, so ritt der Taillefer ins Gefild',
Auf einem hohen Pferde mit Schwert und mit Schild.
Des Herzogs Schwester schaute vom Turm ins Feld;
Sie sprach: „Dort reitet, bei Gott! ein stattlicher Held!" 20

Und als er ritt vorüber an Fräuleins Turm,
Da sang er bald wie ein Lüftlein, bald wie ein Sturm.
Sie sprach: „Der singet, das ist eine herrliche Lust!
Es zittert der Turm, und es zittert mein Herz in der Brust."

Der Herzog Wilhelm fuhr wohl über das Meer, 25
Er fuhr nach Engelland mit gewaltigem Heer.
Er sprang vom Schiffe, da fiel er auf die Hand!
„Hei!—rief er—ich fass' und ergreife dich, Engelland!'

Als nun das Normannenheer im Sturme schritt,
Der edle Taillefer vor den Herzog ritt: 30
„Manch Jährlein hab' ich gesungen und Feuer geschürt,
Manch Jährlein gesungen und Schwert und Lanze gerührt.

„Und hab' ich euch gedient und gesungen zu Dank,
Zuerst als ein Knecht und dann als ein Ritter frank,
So laßt mich das entgelten am heutigen Tag, 35
Vergönnet mir auf die Feinde den ersten Schlag!"

Der Taillefer ritt vor allem Normannenheer
Auf einem hohen Pferde mit Schwert und mit Speer,
Er sang so herrlich, das klang über Hastingsfeld,
Von Roland sang er und manchem frommen Held. 40

Und als das Rolandslied wie ein Sturm erscholl,
Da wallte manch Panier, manch Herze schwoll;
Da brannten Ritter und Mannen von hohem Mut,
Der Taillefer sang und schürte das Feuer gut.

Dann sprengt' er hinein und führte den ersten Stoß, 45
Davon ein englischer Ritter zur Erde schoß;
Dann schwang er das Schwert und führte den ersten Schlag,
Davon ein englischer Ritter am Boden lag.

Normannen sahen's, die harrten nicht allzu lang,
Sie brachen herein mit Geschrei und mit Schilderklang, 50
Hei! sausende Pfeile, klirrender Schwerterschlag,
Bis Harald fiel und sein trotziges Heer erlag.

Herr Wilhelm steckte sein Banner aufs blutige Feld.
Inmitten der Todten spannt' er sein Gezelt.
Da saß er am Mahle, den goldnen Pokal in der Hand, 55
Auf dem Haupte die Königskrone von Engelland.

„Mein tapfrer Taillefer! komm, trink mir Bescheid!
Du hast mir viel gesungen in Lieb' und in Leid;
Doch heut im Hastingsfelde dein Sang und dein Klang,
Der tönet mir in den Ohren mein Lebenlang." 60

XIII. Das Glück von Edenhall.

Von Edenhall der junge Lord
Läßt schmettern Festtrommetenschall,
Er hebt sich an des Tisches Bord
Und ruft in trunkner Gäste Schwall:
„Nun her mit dem Glücke von Edenhall!" 5

Der Schenk vernimmt ungern den Spruch,
Des Hauses ältester Vasall,
Nimmt zögernd aus dem seidnen Tuch
Das hohe Trinkglas von Krystall,
Sie nennen's: Das Glück von Edenhall. 10

Darauf der Lord: „Dem Glas zum Preis
Schenk Roten ein aus Portugal!"
Mit Händezittern gießt der Greis,
Und purpurn Licht wird überall,
Es strahlt aus dem Glücke von Edenhall! 15

Da spricht der Lord und schwingt's dabei:
„Dies Glas von leuchtendem Kryſtall
Gab meinem Ahn am Quell die Fei.
Drein ſchrieb ſie: Kommt dies Glas zum Fall,
Fahr wohl dann, o Glück von Edenhall!

„Ein Kelchglas ward zum Loos mit Fug
Dem freud'gen Stamm von Edenhall;
Wir ſchlürfen gern in vollem Zug,
Wir läuten gern mit lautem Schall!
Stoßt an mit dem Glücke von Edenhall!"

Erſt klingt es milde, tief und voll,
Gleich dem Geſang der Nachtigall,
Dann wie des Waldſtroms laut Geroll;
Zuletzt erdröhnt wie Donnerhall
Das herrliche Glück von Edenhall.

„Zum Horte nimmt ein kühn Geſchlecht
Sich den zerbrechlichen Kryſtall;
Er dauert länger ſchon, als recht,
Stoßt an! mit dieſem kräft'gen Prall
Verſuch' ich das Glück von Edenhall."

Und als das Trinkglas gellend ſpringt,
Springt das Gewölb' mit jähem Knall,
Und aus dem Riß die Flamme bringt;
Die Gäſte ſind zerſtoben all'
Mit dem brechenden Glücke von Edenhall.

Ein ſtürmt der Feind mit Brand und Mord,
Der in der Nacht erſtieg den Wall.
Vom Schwerte fällt der junge Lord,
Hält in der Hand noch den Kryſtall,
Das zerſprungene Glück von Edenhall.

Am Morgen irrt der Schenk allein,
Der Greis, in der zerſtörten Hall,

Er sucht des Herrn verbrannt Gebein,
Er sucht im grausen Trümmerfall
Die Scherben des Glücks von Edenhall. 50

„Die Steinwand,"—spricht er—„springt zu Stück,
Die hohe Säule muß zu Fall,
Glas ist der Erde Stolz und Glück,
In Splitter fällt der Erdenball
Einst gleich dem Glücke von Edenhall." 55

XIV. Des Sängers Fluch.

Es stand in alten Zeiten ein Schloß, so hoch und hehr;
Weit glänzt' es über die Lande bis an das blaue Meer;
Und rings von duft'gen Gärten ein blütenreicher Kranz;
Drin sprangen frische Brunnen in Regenbogenglanz.

Dort saß ein stolzer König, an Land und Siegen reich; 5
Er saß auf seinem Throne so finster und so bleich;
Denn was er sinnt, ist Schrecken, und was er blickt, ist Wut,
Und was er spricht, ist Geißel, und was er schreibt, ist Blut.

Einst zog nach diesem Schlosse ein edles Sängerpaar,
Der Eine in goldnen Locken, der Andre grau von Haar; 10
Der Alte mit der Harfe, der saß auf schmuckem Roß;
Es schritt ihm frisch zur Seite der blühende Genoß.

Der Alte sprach zum Jungen: „nun sei bereit, mein Sohn!
Denk' unsrer tiefsten Lieder, stimm' an den vollsten Ton,
Nimm alle Kraft zusammen, die Lust und auch den Schmerz 15
Es gilt uns heut' zu rühren des Königs steinern Herz."

Schon stehn die beiden Sänger im hohen Säulensaal,
Und auf dem Throne sitzen der König und sein Gemahl;
Der König, furchtbarprächtig, wie blut'ger Nordlichtschein,
Die Königin, süß und milde, als blickte Vollmond drein. 20

Des Sängers Fluch.

Da schlug der Greis die Saiten, er schlug sie wundervoll,
Daß reicher, immer reicher der Klang zum Ohre schwoll;
Dann strömte himmlisch helle des Jünglings Stimme vor,
Des Alten Sang dazwischen, wie dumpfer Geisterchor.

Sie singen von Lenz und Liebe, von sel'ger goldner Zeit,   25
Von Freiheit, Männerwürde, von Treu und Heiligkeit;
Sie singen von allem Süßen, was Menschenbrust durchbebt,
Sie singen von allem Hohen, was Menschenherz erhebt.

Die Höflingsschar im Kreise verlernet jeden Spott,
Des Königs trotz'ge Krieger, sie beugen sich vor Gott;   30
Die Königin, zerflossen in Wehmut und in Lust,
Sie wirft den Sängern nieder die Rose von ihrer Brust.

„Ihr habt mein Volk verführet, verlockt ihr nun mein Weib?"
Der König schreit es wüthend, er bebt am ganzen Leib,
Er wirft sein Schwert, das blitzend des Jünglings Brust durch=
 dringt,   35
Draus, statt der goldnen Lieder, ein Blutstrahl hoch aufspringt.

Und wie vom Sturm zerstoben, ist all der Hörer Schwarm;
Der Jüngling hat verröchelt in seines Meisters Arm.
Der schlägt um ihn den Mantel und setzt ihn auf das Roß,
Er bind't ihn aufrecht feste, verläßt mit ihm das Schloß.   40

Doch vor dem hohen Thore, da hält der Sängergreis,
Da faßt er seine Harfe, sie, aller Harfen Preis;
An einer Marmorsäule, da hat er sie zerschellt,
Dann ruft er, daß es schaurig durch Schloß und Gärten gellt:

„Weh euch, ihr stolzen Hallen! nie töne süßer Klang   45
Durch eure Räume wieder, nie Saite noch Gesang;
Nein! Seufzer nur und Stöhnen und scheuer Sclavenschritt,
Bis euch zu Schutt und Moder der Rachegeist zertritt!

„Weh euch, ihr duft'gen Gärten, im holden Maienlicht!
Euch zeig' ich dieses Toten entstelltes Angesicht,   50

Daß ihr darob verdorret, daß jeder Quell versiegt,
Daß ihr in künft'gen Tagen versteint, verödet liegt.

„Weh dir, verruchter Mörder! Du Fluch des Sängertums!
Umsonst sei all dein Ringen nach Kränzen blut'gen Ruhms;
Dein Name sei vergessen, in ew'ge Nacht getaucht,   55
Sei, wie ein letztes Röcheln, in leere Luft verhaucht!"

Der Alte hat's gerufen, der Himmel hat's gehört;
Die Mauern liegen nieder, die Hallen sind zerstört;
Noch eine hohe Säule zeugt von verschwundner Pracht,
Auch diese, schon geborsten, kann stürzen über Nacht.   60

Und rings statt duft'ger Gärten ein ödes Heideland;
Kein Baum verstreuet Schatten, kein Quell durchdringt den
    Sand;
Des Königs Namen meldet kein Lied, kein Heldenbuch;
Versunken und vergessen! das ist des Sängers Fluch.

XV. Der blinde König. (1804-1814.)

Was steht der nord'schen Fechter Schaar
Hoch auf des Meeres Bord?
Was will in seinem grauen Haar
Der blinde König dort?
Er ruft, in bitterm Harme,   5
Auf seinen Stab gelehnt,
Daß über'm Meeresarme
Das Eiland wiedertönt.

„Gieb, Räuber, aus dem Felsverließ
Die Tochter mir zurück!   10
Ihr Harfenspiel, ihr Lied so süß,
War meines Alters Glück.
Vom Tanz auf grünem Strande
Hast du sie weggeraubt;

Dir ist es ewig Schande,
Mir beugt's das graue Haupt."

Da tritt aus seiner Kluft hervor
Der Räuber, groß und wild;
Er schwingt sein Hünenschwert empor
Und schlägt an seinen Schild.
„Du hast ja viele Wächter,
Warum denn litten's die?
Dir dient so mancher Fechter,
Und keiner kämpft um sie?"

Noch stehn die Fechter alle stumm,
Tritt keiner aus den Reih'n.
Der blinde König kehrt sich um:
„Bin ich denn ganz allein?"
Da faßt des Vaters Rechte
Sein junger Sohn so warm:
„Vergönn' mir's, daß ich fechte!
Wohl fühl ich Kraft im Arm."

„O Sohn! der Feind ist riesenstark,
Ihm hielt noch Keiner Stand.
Und doch! in dir ist edles Mark,
Ich fühl's am Druck der Hand.
Nimm hier die alte Klinge!
Sie ist der Skalden Preis.
Und fällst du, so verschlinge
Die Flut mich armen Greis!"

Und horch! es schäumet und es rauscht
Der Nachen über's Meer;
Der blinde König steht und lauscht,
Und Alles schweigt umher;
Bis drüben sich erhoben
Der Schild und Schwerter Schall
Und Kampfgeschrei und Toben
Und dumpfer Wiederhall.

Da ruft der Greis so freudig bang:
„Sagt an, was ihr erschaut! 50
Mein Schwert, ich kenn's am guten Klang,
Es gab so scharfen Laut."
„Der Räuber ist gefallen,
Er hat den blut'gen Lohn!
Heil dir, du Held vor allen, 55
Du starker Königssohn!"

Und wieder wird es still umher,
Der König steht und lauscht:
„Was hör' ich kommen über's Meer?
Es rudert und es rauscht." 60
„Sie kommen angefahren,
Dein Sohn mit Schwert und Schild,
In sonnenhellen Haaren
Dein Töchterlein Gunild."

„Willkommen!" ruft vom hohen Stein 65
Der blinde Greis hinab:
„Nun wird mein Alter wonnig sein
Und ehrenvoll mein Grab.
Du legst mir, Sohn, zur Seite
Das Schwert von gutem Klang, 70
Gunilde, du Befreite,
Singst mir den Grabgesang."

NOTES.

The references are to *Macmillan's German Course, 2d Year*, and to *Whitney's German Grammar*.

I. Der weiße Hirsch. The white Stag (1811).

1. Birsch (from bürschen), *deer-stalking*.
2. erjagen, to hunt; the prefix er= denotes the successful accomplishment of the action expressed by the verb, as er=leben, *to live to see;* er=listen, *to obtain by cunning*.

    Hirsch, cognate with the English 'hart.'
5. es träumt mir, impers. Verb with the real (logical) subject in the dat.; thus—es ahnt mir, I have a foreboding; cp. Engl. 'it occurs to me'; Fr. 'il me souvient'; Lat. 'licet mihi,' 'libet mihi.'

    klopf, for klopfe, pres. subjunctive for past subj. in indirect quotation; see *M. G. C.*, II., Ex. 6. The apostrophe is, as in English, freely used in poetic diction; cp. l. 13, eh', for ehe.
6. heraus=rauschen, separable comp. verb, *to rush out;* a separable prefix is put at the end of the sentence, when the comp. verb of a principal clause is in a simple tense; so l. 12.

    husch husch! *pop!* an interjection suggestive of noiseless motion; the effect is heightened by the repetition of the sound of sch in rauschte and Hirsch.
7. das Geklaff, or Gekläffe, from klaffen, lit. to gape, to yawn; derived v. kläffen, *to yelp;* hence, as here, *yelping, barking*.
8. brennen, (1) lit. to burn; hence (2) *to fire at*, as here.

    ihm auf das Fell, dat. of pers. pron. + def. art. = possess. pron.; auf sein Fell, quite a common constr. in German; cp. the Fr. lui + le = son; lui + la = sa, etc.

Fell, *skin, hide;* radically akin to the English 'fell,' 'felt,' 'pelt,' and to the Lat. 'pellis.'

piff paff! imitation of the report of a gun: *bang!*

10. ins (in das) Horn stoßen, *to wind the horn* (bugle); lit. to push, *i.e.* to blow, into the horn.

13. gesehn, for gesehn hatten; in a dependent clause the auxil. verb may be left out; see II. 6.

14. davon, here *off and away.*

Höhn, contraction of Höhen, pl. of Höhe, height; Tiefen und Höhn (lit. depths and heights), hill and dale.

II. Einkehr. *The Inn* (1811).

1. wundermild; 'wunder' is used adverbially, *i.e.* wonderfully; for the place of the adj. in poetic diction after the noun, cp. English—'where flourished once a *forest fair*'; thus 'pennon gay,' 'courser proud,' etc.

2. zu Gaste sein bei jemand, *to be some one's guest;* bei, in accordance with its orig. meaning, corresponds to the French 'chez'; so here.

3. der Schild; masc. (1) shield, pl. Schilde; hence (2) das Schild, *sign-board,* as here; plur. Schilder.

6. einkehren, (1) lit. to turn in; (2) to put up; *to take one's quarters;* cp. I. 13.

11. frei, here adverb; nearly all Germ. adjectives may be used adverbially without undergoing any change in form.

12. auf das beste, (auf's beste) absol. superlat.; in *the best manner.*

13. zu; one of the main functions of zu is to denote *purpose, destination,* as here, *for;* cp. *M. G. C.,* II. Ex. 11.

15. zudecken, cp. note to I. 6; er ... selbst is in apposition to Wirt.

17-18. fragt', schüttelt', see note to I. 1. 5.

die Schuldigkeit, *indebtedness;* nach der Sch. fragen, *to ask for one's reckoning;* observe the use of the def. art. instead of the Engl. possess. adj.; thus — Gib mir die Hand (Donnez-moi la main), Give me your hand.

18. Wipfel, *top, crown* (of a tree); and so Gipfel, *top, summit* (of anything: tree, mountain; hence, fig., pitch, pinnacle, zenith, etc.)

NOTES.

III. Die Rache. Retribution (1810).

1. Knecht, akin to the English 'knight,' has had many vicissitudes in the history of its meanings. Starting from its original sense of *boy, youth*, it gradually ascended the social scale from *page* to *squire, warrior, knight* (Anglo-Sax. cnyht, cnëcht), only to sink down again to the abject signification it now has—menial, serf, slave; hence knechten, to enslave; Knechtschaft, servitude, slavery; cp. Trench, *English Past and Pres.*, VII.

2. gern sein, lit. fain (willingly) to be, *i.e. to like to be*.

5. blank, *bright;* frank, adv. *freely;* cp. note to II. l. 1; fr. blank is derived the French 'blanc.'

6. Roß, poet. and provincial for *horse*, to which it is radically akin; Pferd is not originally German, being derived fr. Low Lat. paraveredus, whence Fr. palefroi, O. Fr. palefrei, Engl. palfrey; see Skeat's *Etym. Dict.*

7. sprengen, to gallop, being a derived verb, is conjugated weak, whilst the orig. verb springen, is strong; cp. legen and liegen; fällen and fallen; as a rule the *derived* verb is *transitive*, and the *original* V., *intransitive* in meaning.

9. gülden, archaic form of golden.

IV. Das Schwert. The Sword (1809).

4. erfinden, lit. *to find out*, as here; hence 'to invent,' 'to contrive,' 'to devise,' in which meanings it is generally used now.

5. sich . . . den, dat. of refl. pron. + def. art. = poss. pron.; cp. I. 8.

8. soll geholfen sein, the subject, *i.e.* the impers. pron. es, is understood; lit. *it shall be helped, i.e. remedied; M. G. C.*, Ex. 20.

10. meine, *i.e.* meine Kraft.

11. ihn is object of durchdringt.

V. Siegfried's Schwert. Siegfried's Sword (1812).

1. Siegfried is the chief hero of the Scandinavian National Epos, 'the Edda,' on which the great German epic poem of the 'Nibelungen,' the Iliad of German literature, is founded.

NOTES.

2-4. ging, wollt', supply the subject er.

5. begegnet', used impers.; supply es.
wert; cp. note to II. 1.

8. es ist mir leid, impers. phrase, *it grieves me;* bitter is here similarly constructed.

12. Flammen schlagen, *to blaze; to fly out in sparks.*

17. kunnt', archaic for 'konnte.'

18. Amboß, *anvil*, from 'an,' *on*, and 'bozen' (cogn. with the Engl. 'to butt'), *to smite;* just as in Lat. 'incus' fr. 'incudere.'

21. Eisenstang', comp. of Eisen + stange; here *shaft, lance.* "Compounds are very much more numerous in German than in English, and the liberty of forming new ones, after the model of those already in use, is much more fully conceded than with us. In making practical acquaintance with the language, therefore, we are constantly meeting with them of every class—chance combinations which each speaker or writer forms, as occasion arises, and which are not to be found explained in any dictionary." *Whitney, Germ. Gr.*, § 419. Cp. also VI. 6, VIII. 45, IX. 98, 110, 56, XI. 21, XII. 31, 50, XIII. 2, 13, 21, 49.

VI. Der gute Kamerad. The good Comrade (1809).

This poem, in which Uhland has so well struck the tone of the old popular ballad, has deservedly become one of the most popular songs in Germany.

2. nit, south Germ. for nicht.

6. kam geflogen, past part. for pres. part. after kommen, also after bringen; cp. *M. G. C.*, II. Ex. 15.

7. gilt's = gilt es; gelten, here 'to be aimed at.'

9. mir ... den, dat. of pers. pr. + def. art. = poss. pr.

10. ein Stück von mir, cp. the Lat. 'animae dimidium meae.'

11. will, *i.e.* er will.

12. derweil, archaic for während, *while, whilst.*

13. kann, *i.e.* ich kann.

14. ew'gen for ewigen, dat. sing. neuter of ewig.

VII. **Des Knaben Berglied.** *The Boy's Mountain Song* (1806).

2. bie Schlösser all' = ' all' bie Schlösser.' Cp. note to II. 1.
3. am ersten . . . am längsten, absol. superl., used adverbially—first (longest) of all.
   strahlen (fr. strahl, ray, bolt), *to beam, to shine.*
6. Mutterhaus, *i.e.* Quelle ; *source.*
9. auf=fangen, *to intercept;* the meaning of this line is—I am lord of the stream as well as of the mountain. The same idea is expr. in l. 19 with regard to the storm.
16. Sind Blitz und Donner unter mir ; an allusion to a thunderstorm in a valley as viewed from the top of a mountain. For the inversion of verb and subj., cp. *M. G. C.,* II. p. 102.
17. im Blauen, dat. of das Blaue, from the adj. blau, used substantively.
21. Sturmglock(e), *storm-bell, tocsin,* calling the defenders of the country to arms.
22. manch Feuer auf den Bergen wallt; cp. Schiller's *W. Tell,* II. 2, and V. 1, ' Seht ihr die Feu'rsignale auf den Bergen?' Beacons thus lit on the top of mountains have from times immemorial been used for the purpose of giving the alarm.
23. Glied, (1) lit. limb, member, (2) joint, link, (3) milit. *rank, file.* Ins Glied treten, *to enter the ranks.*

VIII. **Schwäbische Kunde.** *Suabian Lore* (1814).

The emperor of Germany, Frederic I. (of the Hohenstauffen Dynasty), surnamed Rotbart, 'Redbeard,' Lat. Barbarossa, French ' Barberousse,' undertook a crusade in 1188. The incident related here is taken from *Annales Suevici of Crusius,* who had himself drawn it from the Byzantine historian *Nicetas.*

1. lobesam, obsol. derived adj., comp. of lob(e) and =sam (Engl. -some), lit. praiseworthy.
2. gezogen kam, cp. note to VI. 6.
3. mußt' er, this ellipt. use of an auxil. V. is very common in German ; the verb understood is easily supplied from the context ; was soll das (bedeuten)? what does that *mean?* wohin willst du (gehn)? where do you want *to go?*

D

NOTES.

6. viel for viele.
8. ſich (dat.) abthun, -ſich abgewöhnen; to break off a habit, *to wean one's self of.*
9. es iſt mir, impers. Verb, *I feel.*
11. Schwabenland, Suabia, the district inhabited by the 'Suevi,' and called Schwaben until 1495, when it was erected into a duchy under the name of Württemberg; since 1805 a kingdom.
13. des for deſſen. Rößlein, diminut. of 'Roß,' cp. note to III. 6.
14. am, contraction of an dem, *by the.*
16. und koſtet's ihn . . . ; 's for es; the inversion is here = condit. clause; 'und wenn es ihn auch . . . koſtete; so in Engl. 'were it to cost him' for 'if it were to cost him.'
21. huben an, obsol. pret. of anheben.
22. den for ihren; def. art. for poss. pron., cp. II. 18.
23. forcht, in Suabian dialect for fürchtete; so nit for nicht; cp. VI. 2.
24. ſeines Weges, gen. of *manner*, used adverbially; so l. 45.
   Schritt vor (für) Schritt, step by step.
25. ſich . . . den, refl. pron. + def. art. = poss. adj.
26. thät with foll. infinit. is a quaint form for the Preterite; so IX. ll. 32, 60; ſpöttlich for ſpöttiſch, from Spott, scorn, scornfully.
27. dem die Zeit zu lang, supply 'wurde' or 'ward'; die Zeit wird mir lang—time begins to hang heavy upon me.
29. dem Deutſchen ſein Blut, Germ. dat. for the Engl. gen. of the possessor; so l. 31, 32, ihm . . . die.
33. als er . . . gebracht, *i.e.* . . . gebracht hatte, pluperf.; cp. II. 6.
34. da . . . erſt, *then only.*
42. in alle Welt, fig. for *in all directions.*
43. Jedem iſt's, cp. l. 9.
43-44. als würd' ihm . . . geſchnitten —(1) impf. subj. of the impers. passive 'es wird ihm geſchnitten'; (2) a verb with a dat. obj. cannot be used in the personal passive, as is the case in English; cp. 'es iſt mir erlaubt,' Fr. 'il m'est permis,' Lat. 'mihi libitum est.' The inverted constr. with the Verb in the subj. is equivalent to a condit. clause, 'als wenn ihm . . . geſchnitten würde,' so IX. l. 124.

NOTES. 35

45. 'ne, South Germ. for eine.
47. mit gutem Bedacht, deliberately; *at full leisure.*
48. was for 'was für.'
50. der, here pers., and not relat., pron.
    kommen lassen, *to send for;* cp. Fr. faire venir.
52. dich solche Streich' gelehrt; Verbs of teaching, as in Lat. and English, govern a double acc.
54. im Schwange sein, *to be in vogue* (lit. full swing); thus, in den Schwang bringen, *to bring into fashion.*
56. halt, adv. = eben, *forsooth, indeed! you see!*
    Schwaben-streiche; lit. *Suabian pranks,* or *larks.* The inhabitants of Suabia enjoy in Germany very much the same reputation for their Streiche as the Irish in these islands for their 'bulls.'

IX. Klein Roland. *Little Roland* (1808).

For the original of this ballad, Uhland is indebted to the Spanish 'Noches de Inuierno' (winternights) by 'Antonio de Esclava,' published early in the seventeenth century; according to that Selection of Tales, *Bertha,* the fair sister of Charlemagne, had incurred his displeasure for having secretly married a poor knight, Milo of Anglante (X. 15). Having fled to Italy to escape his wrath, she gave birth to Roland (Ital. Orlando) in a cavern near Siena. The events here related are supposed to have happened on the occasion of Charlemagne's passage through that town on his return from Rome. The original version has not been altogether literally followed by Uhland.

3. in freier Luft, *in the open air;* thus 'unter freiem Himmel.'
5. hehr (old comparat. of hoch, höher), *lofty, august.* O, here *alas!*
7. Um, *for the sake of;* cp. ums Himmels Willen, for heaven's sake.
10. verschlang mir dich; mir, dat. of the person after a verb of *taking.* In this ballad Milo is supposed to have been drowned whilst crossing a torrent. We see him, however, reappear in the next ballad.
11. die, relat. pr. referring to 'mich' in next line; mich . . . die ich, after a relat. pr. referring to a pers. pron. in the 1st

or 2d p., this pr. is repeated; cp. 'Das wissen wir, die wir die Gemsen jagen.' Schiller's *W. Tell*, I. 1.

14. Ehr' und Liebe mir, dat. of pers. pron. for possess. adj., thou my honour and thou my love!

20. dem, dat. sing. of pers. pron.; der, *he;* cp. note to VIII. l. 50; so die, ll. 31, 113.

21. zur Tafel, *i.e.* zu Tische; we should say—an (bei) der Tafel sitzen.

22. Rittersaal, lit. knightly hall; here *banquet-hall.*

26. ward, pret. of werden; this stem is used in the sing. only.

30. der Bettler, gen. pl. depending on 'viel,' here used substantively, so l. 85.

35-6. drückt sich herfür, lit. 'squeezes himself forward,' *i.e. pushes (elbows) his way.*

37. wunderbar, for wunderlich, *strange, odd;* wunderbar means wonderful, wondrous, which is not the sense intended here.

38. vierfarb for vierfarbig; lit. *four-coloured, motley;* zusammen stücken, *to patch together.*

41. hereintreten zu; notice the peculiar use of zu with verbs of motion:—zum Fenster hineinfliegen, to fly in 'by' the window, so l. 98.

43. von Tisches Mitt'; in prose we should say—von der Mitte des Tisches; so l. 61, von Königs Tisch, for von des Königs Tisch.

44. stumm, lit. dumb, here adv., *in silence; without saying a word.*

45. muß here expresses astonishment: *do I see aright?*

46. sondrer, nom. masc. sing. of sonder, obsol. as adj., for sonderbar, *strange;* so l. 82.

47. es geschehen lassen, lit. to let it happen, *i.e. to allow it.*

49. stund . . . an; obsol. for stand . . . an, pret. of anstehen; here *to last.*

50. kehrt, for kehrt zurück.

53. heida! interjection, *stop!* Wicht, akin to the Engl. 'wight;' here *imp.* Wicht is one of those numerous terms which have seen better days, like Knecht (cp. III. l. 1), Buhle; the orig. meaning is—thing, being, creature; in composition—Bösewicht, miscreant.

57. sehen; here *to look.*

64. Weines Schaum, for schäumenden Wein, *sparkling wine.*

NOTES.   37

67. Wildbret, and not Wildpret, as sometimes spelt; comp. of Wild and Braten, lit. game roast, *i.e. roast game.*
68. ihr, *i.e.* ihr ziemet.
70. berühmen (sich), rather unusual for sich rühmen, *to boast.*
71. lustsam, unusual for reizend; Schloß lustsam = Lustschloß.
73. Truchseß, *lord high steward;* Schenk (fr. schenken, to pour out for drinking), here = Mundschenk, *cup-bearer.*
78. allstund, archaic for allemal or immerdar, *evermore.*
79. frei, here *blithe.*
85. der Knaben; gen. plur. depending on acht; cp. note to l. 30.
87. Zins (fr. Lat. census); rent, tax, interest; here *tribute.*
88. vierfältig; lit. fourfold; cp. l. 38, *i.e. four kinds of . . .*
    Wat, obsol. for cloth, clothes; akin to Wand in Leinwand, old form: Lînwât.
91. wohl, like several other adverbs doch, ja, auch, schon, gern, etc., is often best rendered by a verb; here *I guess;* see l. 143.
98. Prunkgemach; comp. of Prunk, pomp, parade, state, and Gemach, room; so l. 111. Prunksaal, comp. of Prunk + saal, *hall.*
    zum; cp. note, l. 41.
106. hilf Himmel! *heaven help me!*
113. zu Füßen ihm, dat. of pers. pr. for possess. pron.; cp. note to ll. 20, 31.
114. das bleiche Frauenbild; in appos. to Frau Bertha, l. 113; Bild often thus enters in compos. in the sense of 'person,' 'figure'; so Weibsbild, vulg. for female; Mannsbild, man, Sternbild, constellation; so l. 130.
120. Ohm or Ohme, contract. of Oheim, *uncle,* has in course of time given way to Onkel (from Fr. oncle, Lat. avunculus), just as Muhme has been all but dispossessed by Tante, and Base by Cousine.
124. dir verziehen sein, cp. note to VIII., ll. 43, 44.
128. Guts for Gutes, adj. used as subst.; the inflection es is originally the genitive-ending, here depending on was; thus—Etwas Neues (Lat. 'quid novi,' Fr. 'quelque chose de nouveau').
129, 131-3-5. soll, *i.e.* er soll.

130. Hetbenbitb, cp. note to l. 114.

131. die Farb von manchem Reich, allusion to his garment; see ll. 38 and 88.

135. frei, here *daring*.

136. seufzend Mutterland, alluding to the frequent inroads of the Saracens; the meaning of Roland, orig. Ruodland, is 'glory of the land.'

X. Roland Schildträger. *Roland the Shield-Bearer* (1811).

This ballad is not founded on any tradition, but was composed by Uhland under the influence of his intimate studies of the legendary lore concerning Roland stored up in Old French literature.

2. Aachen, *Aix-la-Chapelle*; fr. Lat. *aquas*, waters, watering-place; hence 'Aix' has become the name for several watering-places; so Aachen, on account of its sulphurous springs. In the early middle ages it was the favourite residence of the Frankish kings, especially of Charlemagne; he died and was buried there (814 A.D.)

3. Wildbret und Fisch, cp. note to l. 67.

5. Goldgeschirr; Geschirr is the name for any kind of utensil, gear, tackle, tackling, harness, earthenware, *plate*, as here.

9. sollen is often thus used elliptically; supply bedeuten; cp. note to VIII. 3.

11. uns is in the dat. case, depending on fehlen; constr. like Fr. 'falloir' and 'faillir.'

13. im Schilde sein, poet. and quaint for in seinem Schilde; so ll. 50, 52.

14. Ardennerwalde, and l. 30. Ardennen, the same forest of *Arden* in which the scene of Shakspeare's *As You Like It* is laid.

15-18. Graf Richard (of Normandy), Erzbischof Turpin (archbishop of Rheims), Herr Haimon, Naims (Naims) von Baiern, Milon von Anglant, and Graf Garin (Guerin of Lorraine); six of the twelve champions of Charlemagne, celebrated by the cyclus of epic poems (*Chansons de Gestes*) which has gathered round the person of that powerful monarch; cp. the next ballad.

19. sie haben begehrt, this use of the pres. perf. for the preterite is unusual.

NOTES.

Stahlgewand, lit. steel garment, *i.e. armour.*
20. hießen, impf. of heißen, here *to order.*
22. Jung Roland, Sohn des Milon ; see the preceding ballad.
24. vermeint ihr mich; inversion = condit. clause.
27. euch is in the dat. case.
32. thäten, see note to VIII. l. 26.
33. hinterm, contract. of hinter dem, *i.e.* seinem.
herreiten, *to ride along.*
34. wie wohl ihm war ; preterite of the impers. phrase—es ist ihm wohl, *he takes delight in,* cp. viii., l. 9.
37. Degen, a warrior, champion (akin to Engl. thane ; for the loss of *g,* cp. Regen = rain, Wagen = wain); Degen, sword, is of quite different origin : from Fr. 'dague.'
39. das Gehege (from hegen, to hedge in), means properly, fence, inclosure, preserve for game, etc.; here it is taken in the sense of *copse.*
41. schlafen lag, archaic use of the infinitive after liegen.
45. davon die, for the gen. dessen.
48. den, here demonstr. pron.
50. gedacht' for dachte ; gedenken is generally used in the sense of (1) to remember, to mention, to bear in mind ; hence (2) to intend, to be about.
51. was . . . für ein . . . , *what a* . . . ; this peculiar phrase (which once was used in English) is often thus separated by the verb and its Predicate.
54. es wachet, lit. there watches, there is awake ; this impers. use of a verb is very common in Germ. ; cp. es lächelt der See, etc. Schiller's *Tell,* I. 1.
57. zur Seite binden, *to gird.*
58. Herrn Milons starkes Waffen, in apposition to Schwert; das Waffen here neuter, the gender it had in Old G. ; now fem. die Waffe ; so l. 165.
60. that . . . aufraffen, cp. note to VIII. l. 26.
62. der Tann, *i.e.* Tannenwald, *pine-wood.*
66. Fant (radically connected with 'infant'), *lad, stripling.*
68. zwier, obsol. for zweifach, *twice.*

NOTES.

69. ſchier, South Germ. for faſt or beinahe : *well-nigh, almost.*

73. hab' ich die Tartſche lang und breit; (1) hab' ich, inversion = concess. clause ; (2) for the constr. ich hab' die T. lang, cp. the Fr. 'j'ai la targe longue'; (3) Tartſche, *shield*, is an instance of a Germ. word acclimatised on French soil and returning to its native land under a foreign garb ; the Old Germ. is 'zarga,' Low Lat. 'targa,' Fr. 'targe'; thus 'bivouac' from Beiwache, 'amüſiren' from 'amuser,' and this from Muße.

78. Stange, *i.e.* Speer; (1) lit. pole, perch, shaft ; hence (2) *lance*, as here.

83. Wunderſchilde, *magic shield.*

88. unbehende, lit. unhandy ; hence *awkward, clumsy ;* from behende (fr. Hand), lit. handy, nimble, quick.

92. dem Rieſen ſchwand der Muth, dat. of pers. instead of gen. of the possessor ; see note to IX. 113.

   dahin ſchwinden, *to quail.*

93. Wie ihm der Schild entriſſen (supply war, cp. II. 6)—(1) wie, here *as soon as ;* (2) ihm, dat. of remoter obj. after verbs of *taking ;* as in Fr. 'lui fut arraché.'

94. verliehen, *i.e.* verliehen hatte, cp. note to II. 6.

100. hieb ihm das Haupt herunter, dat. of pers. pr. + def. art. = possess. pron., Haupt, poet. for Kopf.

106. unterm, contraction of unter dem.

107. der Quell = die Quelle.

108. ſich . . . Gewand und Waffen, dat. of reflex. pron. instead of possess. pron.

109. helle for rein, here used predicatively to wuſch.

116. aufgeſprungen, supply war ; cp. II. 6.

119. ſuchen, here pres. subj., to express *purpose.*

121. die Wilde for die Wildnis, *wilderness.*

123. deſſen (Lat. ejus), instead of ſeinem, to avoid the ambiguity ; cp. *M. G. C.*, II. § 29 (5), Obs.

125. hätt', quaint for hatte ; so that for that, VII. l. 26, and above, l. 32.

128. war zu ſchauen ; observe the use of *active* inf. with zu instead of the Engl. *passive :—was to be seen.*

NOTES. 41

129. baju, being logically connected with nicht, l. 128, is here = noch, *nor.*
130. so, here archaic form of relat. pron., *which.*
132. auch nicht, *nor.*
135. cp. notes to l. 51, and VIII. l. 45.
136. man sieht am, *one can see by;* zerhaunen, contract. of zerhauenen.
138. Frag ich mehr? *need I ask more?*
139. Verschlafen, past part., *to sleep away;* the force of the pref. ver= is the same as that of the cognate Engl. *fore* in *to forego,* implying that through the action denoted by the verb the object aimed at is not obtained (forfeited).
141. stund, archaic for stand.
143. wohl, cp. note to l. 91 ; here, *I wonder if . . .*
144. allzu lange; all and aller are often thus used to strengthen an adjective, especially the superlative, as allerliebst.
147. des Riesen Haupt am Speere; Haupt, acc. absol. used as an adv. phrase; supply an appropriate verb, as *bearing,* or a prep.: *with.* Cp. He advanced *sword in hand,* Fr. 'l'épée à la main.'
148. in trübem Muth, *i.e.* in Trübsinn, *downcast.*
151. dem König vor die Füße, dat. of the pers. concerned, instead of the gen. of possessor ; cp. note to ix., l. 113.
152. der Hag, in the sense of its derivative Gehege, l. 39, *i.e. copse, wood.*
157. ungefüg for ungeschlacht, *uncouth.*
159. Reliquienstück, lit. *piece of relic.*
161. zu=hauen, *to rough-hew, to dress.*
167. Bairisch(es) Bier, nom. in apposition to Schluck; as we say, ein Stück Brot. Several towns in Bavaria enjoy the same reputation in Germany as Burton-on-Trent in England.
168. munden; notice the constr., *i.e.* the name of the thing relished in the nom., and the person who relishes in the dat.
169. daher=kommen, *to come along.*
171. die Wehr, collective, *weapons.*
175. ist, *i.e.* es ist.
178. des, gen. of demonstrative (here pers.) pron. used for possess. pron. : *his.*

181. hätt' ich gern, pret. (impf.) subjunctive for condit. pres. würde (möchte) ich gern haben.
184. lenkte, i.e. fein Pferd.
185. ließ . . . gehn; cp. note to VIII. 50.
188. ihm, dat. of advantage ; *for him.*
189. zusammt, obsol. for sammt, *together with.*
190-1. kamen geritten; cp. note to VI. 6.
192. losmachen, *to take off.*
193. in der Mitten; Mitten, old dat. of die Mitte; fem. nouns in *e* used to take n in the oblique case of the sing.
196. die liebe Sonne; liebe frequently a merely ornamental epithet, freely used in German, where in English it hardly admits of translation ; so—das liebe Leben; liebe Zeit! der liebe Gott.
202-3. ihm abgeschlagen, ihm entriffen; cp. note to l. 100.
209. Wicht, see note to IX. l. 53.

XI. König Karl's Meerfahrt. Charlemagne's Sea-Voyage (1812).

It is almost needless to say that Charlemagne never undertook a pilgrimage to the Holy Land. But if we bear in mind the religious enthusiasm that pervaded the period to which most old French poems relating to him owe their origin, and which ultimately led to the Crusades, we can easily understand how it is that the greatest hero of Christendom has been credited with this act of devotion. According to the ideas of those times, no Christian hero could possibly be conceived as not having made a pilgrimage to the Holy Sepulchre.

2. Genossen (from pret. stem of genießen, *i.e.* genoß), companion ; here *peer*, fr. Fr. 'pair'; see note to X. 15-18.
6. schirmen, to protect, to screen (cp. Regenschirm; Schirmvogt), *to fence,* as here.
7. Stand halten, to be proof.
9. Holger aus Dänemark, in old Fr., Ogier le Danois.
11. helfen; here *to avail.*
12. jagen, lit. to hunt, to chase ; here, to roll, to swell, to surge.
13. Oliver, old Fr. Olivier, Comte de Gennes, to whose famous single fights with Roland on an island of the Rhone we owe the proverb, ' A Roland for an Oliver.'

15. **es ist mir um,** I care for; fo, here *so much;* hence—**es ist mir um mich selbst nicht so,** *it is not so much about myself I care.*
16. **Alteklâre,** from the Fr. 'haute-claire' (tall and bright), the name of Oliver's battlesword, in accordance with the custom of ancient chivalry; thus Roland's mighty sword with which he could cleave· rocks, bore the name of *Durandal,* that of Charlemagne *Joyeuse;* cp. the name of King Arthur's brand 'Excalibur.'
17. **schlimm,** here *treacherous;* it was 'Ganelon' who afterwards, according to tradition, betrayed Roland into the hands of the Saracens at Roncevaux, a defile in the Pyrenees.
19. **war ich mit guter Art davon;** inverted constr. = condit. clause, see VIII. 1. 43, *were I safely off.*
21. **Turpin,** Archbishop of Rheims.
25. **Richard Ohnefurcht** (sans-peur), Duke, here called Graf, of Normandy.
29. **Naimis, Naimes,** Duke of Bavaria.
33. **Riol,** of 'le Mans.'
37. **Gui,** Guy de Bourgoyne.
41. **Garin,** Garin, Guérin, Duke of Lorraine.
42. **die Schwere;** lit. heaviness; here, *difficulty.*
45. **Lambert,** Prince of Brussels.
49. **Gottfried,** Geoffroy, Seigneur de Bourdelois.
   lobesan, poetic form of **lobesam;** cp. V. 1.
50. **es sich gefallen lassen,** *to submit to it;* **sich** is in the dative.
55. **mit festem Maß,** *with firm grasp* (lit. measure).

XII. Taillefer. (1812.)

The original source of this poem is to be found in the *Roman de Rou,* an old epic poem in Norman-French, which treats of the Norman Conquest—

> "Taillefer, ki mult bien cantout,
> Sor un cheval ki tost alout,
> Devant li Dus alout cantant
> De Karlemaine è de Rollant,[1]
> E d'Oliver è des vassals
> Ki moururent en Rencheyals." . . .

[1] Cp. IX. and X.

4. mir das Herz; cp. note to I. 8.
5. der so gerne singt; cp. note to III. 3; gerne is best rendered by a verb, *to like to, to be fond of*.
17. nicht lange, *before long;* das Gefild(e), collective form of Feld, field ; cp. Hag and Gehege, X. l. 39.
22. Lüftlein, diminut. of Luft, *breeze*.
24. es zittert; cp. note to X. 54:—
in der Brust, def. art. for poss. pr.; so l. 27.
26 and 28. Engelland, the old form for England.
"In egressu navis pede lapsus, eventum in melius commutavit, acclamante sibi proximo milite : Tenes, inquit, Angliam, comes, rex futurus." Guil. Malmesburiensis, Gesta regum Angl., III. § 238.
30. In prose we should here place the verb first, this principal clause being preceded by a dependent clause.
31. Jährlein, unusual diminut. of Jahr; cp. note to V. l. 6.
33. zu Dank, *to your satisfaction*.
34. ein Ritter frank, *a free knight*.
35. einen (or einem) entgelten lassen, generally to make one pay (suffer) for ; here in a good sense, *to reward, to requite*.

> "Sires, dist Taillefer, merci,
> Jo vos ai lungement servi,
> Tut mon servise me debvez ;
> Hui se vost plaist me le rendez
> Por tut guerredun vos requier,
> E si vos voil forment préier ;
> Otréiez mei, ke jo n'i faille,
> Li primier colp de la bataille."
> ROMAN DE ROU.

37. vor allem, *i.e.* vor all dem, or vor dem ganzen.
40. von Roland sang er; see introductory notice above.
42. Herze, the Old Germ. form (old gen. Herzen, now Herzens, or Herzes), cognate with Lat. cor, cordis, so that the Engl. *cordial* and *hearty* are virtually akin.
43. Mannen, plur. of Mann, in the sense of *warriors, retainers*, see l. 43.
49. Normannen; supply the def. art.
55. den goldnen Pokal, absol. acc. used as adv. phrase ; cp. note to X. 147.

NOTES. 45

55-56. in der Hand, auf dem Haupt, def. art. for poss. adj.; in what case is die Königskrone?

57. Bescheid trinken (or thun), *to pledge one*.

58. in Lieb' und in Leid; alliteration, *in joy* (lit. love) *and sorrow*.

60. der is here a pers. pron., relating the complex subject dein Sang und dein Klang, l. 59, treated as singular, because Sang and Klang are synonymous.

XIII. Das Glück von Edenhall. The Luck of Edenhall (1834).

Imitated from *Ritson's Fairy Tales*. According to an old tradition, a curiously-wrought cup of red crystal was given by a fairy to an ancestor of the Musgrave family of Edenhall in Cumberland. The glass, which is still in possession of that family, has the following verse engraven on it:—
" If this glass do break or fall,
Farewell the luck of Edenhall."
Hence its name. It will be seen that Uhland has not strictly followed the original tradition, according to which the precious cup was saved from wreck by the presence of mind of the steward. Comp. also the ballad "The Luck of Muncaster," a glass cup presented to the Pennington family by King Henry VI., who had found shelter in Muncaster (Mealcastre) Castle (1461).

2. läßt schmettern; notice the use of the *active* infinit. after lassen, as after 'faire' in French.

Trommeten, poetical form of Trompeten.

4. Schwall, lit. swell, rising waves; here *revelry*.

5. her mit, ellipt. for Kommt her mit, lit. come hither with, *i.e. bring*.

6-7. Schenk ... Vasall; with this cp. the ominous forebodings of Terzky's butler in Schiller's *Wallenstein* (II. *The Piccolominis*), IV. 5; l. 7 stands in apposition to Schenk.

11. dem Glas zum Preis, *in honour* (lit. praise) *of* the glass.

12. Roten, *i.e.* roten Wein.

14. wirb, here *spreads, streams*.

16. schwingt's, *i.e.* es = das Glas.

18. Quell, m.; Quelle, f.; cp. note to X. 107.

Fei, Fee (from Fr. fée, Lat. fatum); cp. the Engl. form *fay* and *fairy*.

19-20. See Introductory Notice.

21. zum Loos werden, *to fall to the lot;* ward, cp. note to IX. l. 26. mit Fug, with good reason; here *deservedly*.

29. erdröhnen, or dröhnen, to roar, to rumble.

31. Hort, akin to 'hoard'; here *charm, palladium*.

32. sich is here the dat. of advantage.

33. dauert schon, Germ. pres. for Engl. pres. perf.; see *M. G. C.*, II. Ex. 1.

36. gellen, *to resound;* cognate with 'to yell'; cp. also Nachtigall, nightingale.

37. jäh, jähe (older form jâch, gâh, gâhe), implies abruptness, both in time and space; here *sudden*.

39. zerstoben, insep. comp. of zer + stieben (stob, gestoben), akin to Staub, stäuben, 'dust'; hence its meaning—*to be scattered as dust, to fly to dust;* the force of the prefix zer is, as a rule, that of dispersion; zer is akin to the Lat. *dis*.

47. der Greis, in apposition to Schenk.

49. Trümmerfall, a compound coined by Uhland; cp. note to V. 21.

51. zu Stück springen, *to fall to pieces*.

52. muß, elliptical form for muß kommen; cp. note to VIII. 3.

53. Glas, etc., cp. the prov.—„Glück und Glas,
  Wie bald bricht das!"

XIV. Des Sängers Fluch. The Minstrel's Curse (1814).

For the subject of this ballad the poet, as in the case of Roland Schildträger (VII.), has entirely drawn upon his own imagination.

1. hoch und hehr, an expressive phrase, alliterative in form, and graduated in meaning; hoch denoting the *physical* feature and hehr the commanding aspect of the castle; hehr, lit. awe-inspiring; hence der Herr, the lord.

2. die Lande, poetical, instead of the more usual Länder.

3. Supply the verb war; von duft'gen (contr. of duftigen) Gärten depends on Kranz.

NOTES.

4. drin, contract. of darin; cp. l. 20—drein for darein.
7. blicken, here used transitively.
11. der faß auf schmuckem Roß; it was customary in the golden age of minstrelsy for minstrels to ride from court to court, from castle to castle; cp. also W. Scott's *Lay of Last Minstrel*—"No more on prancing palfrey borne
He carolled light as lark at morn."
14. denken, constructed in poetic diction with the gen., instead of an with acc.

tief, here *heart-stirring*.

stimmen, to tune; anstimmen, lit. to begin to tune, *to strike up*, to intonate.
15. zusammen=nehmen, *to gather, to summon, to muster up;* sich zusammen=nehmen, *to collect one's thoughts*.

die Lust und auch den Schmerz, *the accents of bliss and sorrow*.
16. gelten, to be worth; here used impers. in the sense of the Fr. 'il s'agit de,' Lat. 'agitur,' *the question is, our task is to* . . .
18. das Gemahl, *i.e.* die Gemahlin; the use of neuter nouns to denote females is not at all uncommon in Germ.; cp. das Weib, das Weibsbild, das Frauenzimmer, das Mensch, and, of course, all diminutives: das Mädchen, etc.
19. furchtbar is adv., qualifying prächtig.

blut'ger contr. of blutig=er, here *blood-red*, referring to his garments, for his face is described in l. 6 as ghastly pale.
20. drein blicken, as distinguished from blicken, is suggestive of the expression of the look.
21. Da schlug der Greis die Saiten, cp. *Lay of Last Minstrel*—'He swept the sounding chords along.'
24. dazwischen, *i.e.* dazwischen tönend, *falling in*.
25. Lenz, archaic, and now poet., for Frühling, *spring;* akin to English 'Lent.'
26. Männerwürde; Männer, here used as adj.: *manly worth, manliness.*
27. was, relat. pr., referring to an indef. pron. antecedent, *i.e.* alles.

beben, lit. to wave; hence, to quiver, to shake; durch=beben, *to thrill through*.
29. verlernen, *to unlearn;* the force of the pref. ver, like that of

its Engl. cognate *fore* in forego, *forswear*, is explained in note VII. 140; cp. also l. 33.

30. troꜩ'ge for troꜩige.
36. brauß, contr. of barauß.
    Blutſtrahl; Strahl, here *stream, gush, torrent, jet, spurt*.
38. verröcheln, lit. 'to cease rattling in the throat,' fig. *to breathe one's last*, as here; cp. l. 56, verhauchen.
40. bind't, a rather strong contraction of bindet, for the sake of the metre.
42. ſie, aller Harfen Preiß, lit. the prize of all harps, *i.e. the harp of harps*.
42-3. ſie, in apposition to Harfe.
45. töne, 3d p. sing. of imperative.
46. Saite, *i.e.* Harfe; a metonymy, part for the whole, as 'sail' for 'ship.'
49. Maienlicht, comp. of Mai (month of May) and Licht.
51. darob, poetic for darüber, lit. thereover, *i.e. over it, through it*.
53. Sängertum, an unusual compound: *minstrelsy*.
60. kann, here *may*.

XV. Der blinde König. The blind King (1804, recast 1814).

For the chief incidents of this ballad, one of Uhland's earliest attempts,—he was only seventeen when he first composed it—the young poet was indebted to *Saxo Grammaticus*, a Danish historian, who lived in the twelfth century and wrote the history of Denmark in Latin (*Historia Danica*).

There it is related that *Wermund*, the old blind king of Denmark, was challenged by a king of Saxony either to resign his crown, or, failing this, to let their two sons meet in single combat to decide which was the worthiest successor to the Danish throne.

Wermund declares he is ready to meet the Saxon king himself; but the heralds spurn the idea of such an unequal combat, he being stricken in years and blind, when suddenly a voice is heard from the ranks of the Danes, accepting the challenge and declaring that there was one Dane ready to meet not only the Saxon king's son but another champion to boot. To the surprise of all, this turns out to be the Danish king's son *Uffo*, who

NOTES. 49

up to that day had passed for dumb and imbecile—a fact on which the wily Saxon king had relied for the successful issue of his challenge. Uffo, having succeeded in overcoming his father's misgivings, is entrusted with the trusty blade *Skrep*, which the king had long since buried in the ground, no one being deemed worthy to wield it after him. The combat takes place, and both the Saxon king's son and the giant champion attending him are killed.

It will be seen that Uhland has not by any means strictly adhered to his original.

1. was for warum? so in Shakspeare, *what* for *why?* "The occasional use of questions gives life and energy to style. Hence we find them both in poetry and rhetoric. In poetry they heighten the dramatic effect by bringing the supposed scene more vividly before us." See notes to *The Lay of the Last Minstrel*, Phillpotts' edit.

    Fechter, in Saxo Grammaticus 'athleta.'

2. Bord is used both in the masc. and neuter.

6. gelehnt, passive part. for active pres. part. ; so Bediente, servant ; cp. English *propped = leaning*.

8. Eiland ; this archaic and poetical term for *island* is strictly cognate with the English word, whilst the more usual Insel is derived from the Lat. 'insula.' It was an old Scandinavian custom to fight single combats in islands, hence called *Holmgang*. Thus also Roland and Oliver fought on an island of the Rhone ; cp. note to XI. 13.

9. Verließ, from verlieren, Old Germ. verliesen, *i.e.* losing itself in the ground ; lit. dungeon, keep ; Felsverließ, *rocky cave*.

10. die . . . mir, and l. 16, mir . . . das, see note to X. l. 100.

19. Hünenschwert (from Hunne, Hun) ; der Hüne, warrior giant ; hence Hünengrab, barrow.

29. die Rechte, *i.e.* die rechte Hand ; whilst das Recht = the right (in the abstract).

32. im Arm, cp. note to I. l. 8.

35. das Mark, lit. *marrow, pith, sap*, symbol of strength ; hence markig, pithy ; proverb. expression :—Mark in den Knochen haben, *to be stalwart ;* die Mark, (1) marches, *i.e.* borders ; (2) weight (of precious metals) ; (3) a coin = one shilling.

36. fühlen an, to feel by ; one of the main functions of an is to express, as here, the test, the means, by which we arrive

E

at a conclusion; man sieht es ihm an den Augen an, it is easy to see by his eyes.

37. die alte Klinge, lit. the old blade, *i.e.* here, his sword Skrep, Scandinavian for *smooth*, which, according to Saxo, the king had buried in the ground, but unearthed again for this fight; cp. note to XI. l. 16.

38. der Skalde, the old Scandinavian word for *bard;* aller Skalden Preis, cp. note to XIV. l. 42.

41. es schäumet und es rauscht; and l. 60; cp. note to X. l. 54.

45. sich erhoben, cp. note to X. l. 54.

46. der Schild, cp. note to II. l. 3.

49. freudig bang, *i.e.* joyful (freudig) at hearing the old familiar clanging of his trusty sword, and yet anxious (bang) about the issue of the fight.

61. sie kommen angefahren; for part. perf. after kommen, cp. note to VI. l. 6.

69. mir zur Seite, cp. note to X. l. 100. "The blindness and helplessness of the father, his distress, his anguish for his daughter, his fear for his son, his instinct of confidence in a good cause and a young courage, are all finely indicated, almost without a thought of description; but if we could put ourselves for a moment in a blind man's place, under such circumstances as the ballad sets forth, we should find no truer idea of the very climax of anxiety than that expressed in the awful silence which follows the rippling of the departing boat when its sound is lost in the distance before the strife begins."—*Quarterly Review*, No. 231.

VOCABULARY.

ABBREVIATIONS.

acc. = accusative.
adj. = adjective.
adv. = adverb.
advl. = adverbial.
art. = article.
cogn. = cognate.
comp., or cp. = compare.
comp. of = composed of.
conj. = conjunction.
contr. = contraction.
dat. = dative.
def. = definite.
Engl. = English.
f. = feminine.
fr. = from.
Fr. = French.
gen. = genitive.
gov. = governing.
imperat. = imperative.
indicat. = indicative.

insep. = inseparable.
irr. = irregular.
m. = masculine.
n. = neuter.
numb. = number.
O. E. = Old English.
obsol. = obsolete.
p. = page.
p.p. = past (perf.) participle.
pers. = person.
pl. = plural.
pr. = pronoun.
prep. = preposition.
pres. = present.
reflex. = reflexive.
subj. = subjunctive.
trans. = transitive.
v. = verb.
* = cognate with German.

The figures refer to the respective number of each Ballad, and to the lines (not to the pages); thus—VIII. 8 placed after *to wean one's self of*, indicates that fich abthun in the 8th line of the 8th Ballad is to be rendered by that word.

If no number is given, the English words in italics may be considered correct equivalents to a German word wherever it occurs.

English words marked with an * are cognate with the German words defined.

To each *masculine* or *neuter* noun are added the inflections of the genit. sing. and nominat. plur.

To each *feminine* noun is added the inflection of the nominat. plur.

The sign " indicates modification of the stem-vowel.

The absence of the plural inflection implies that the plural is wanting or unusual.

The hyphen (-) between the prefix and stem of a compound verb indicates that it is *separable*.

VOCABULARY.

A

Aachen, Aix-la-Chapelle [fr. Lat. aquas; see note, p. 38].
Abend=zeit, f., *even*tide, evening.*
abends, adv., *in the evening.*
ab=geschlagen, p.p. of ab=schlagen, *to cut off.*
ab=gethan, p.p. of ab=thun; see note, p. 34.
ab=hauen (hieb ... ab, ab=gehauen), *to cut (hew*) off,* VIII. 31.
ab=thun (that ... ab, ab=gethan), lit. *to do* off**, *i.e. to give up;* refl., *to wean one's self of,* VIII. 8; see note, p. 34.
acht, *eight*.*
Acht, f., *attention, heed, care,* V. 15.
Ahn(e), =s(=n), =en, m., *ancestor.*
all, adj., *all**, IV. 9; *every.*
allein, adv., *alone*.*
allezeit (comp. of alle, *all**, and Zeit, *time*), *at all times, evermore.*

allstund, obsol. adv., *evermore.*
allzu, adv., *too*;* see note, p. 41.
als, advl. conj., *when,* VIII. 1.
als, conj., *as*, when;* after a compar. *than.*
als wie, adv., *just as.*
also, adv., *so; thus;* conj., *so then.*
alt, adj. or adv., *old*.*
Alte, =n, =n, m., *old man.*
Alteklâre, f., see note, p. 43.
Alter, =s, n., *old age.*
am, contr. of an=dem, *by the,* VIII. 14; XV. 51; *on the,* X. 147, 156; XIII. 46.
Amboß, =es, =e, m., *anvil;* see note, p. 32.
an, prep. gov. acc. or dat., *on**, II. 4; *by,* VI. 4; X. 136.
an=blicken, *to stare at.*
ander, plur. and(e)re, *other*,* V. 24.
Ander(es), n. subst., *something else;* nichts anders, *no worse fate,* XI. 51.

VOCABULARY.

Anderer, m., *other, some one else.*
an=fangen (fing . . . an, ange= fangen), *to begin.*
an=gefahren, p.p. of an=fahren, *to arrive ; to row near (on).*
Angesicht, =s, =er, n., *face, visage, countenance.*
an=halten, *to stop.*
an=heben (hob or hub . . . an, an=gehoben), *to begin; to set to.*
an=legen, *to put on ; to don.*
an=richten, *to prepare ;* fam., *to dish up.*
an=schauen, *to look at (on).*
an=stehen (stund . . . an), *to last.*
an=stimmen, *to strike up.*
an=stoßen, *to touch glasses; to clink;* to hob-nob.
Apfel, =s, ″=, m., *apple*.
Apfelbaum, =es, ″=e, m., *appletree.*
Arbeit, =en, f., *work.*
Ardenner=wald, =es, m., *Forest of Arden ;* see note, p. 38.
Arm, =es, =e, m., *arm*.
Art, =en, f., kind, manner ; mit guter Art davon, *safely off,* XI. 19.
Ast, =es, ″=e, m., *bough, branch.*
äß(e), first p. sing. pret. subj. of essen (aß, gegessen), *to eat*.

auch, adv., *also.*
auch nicht, adv., *nor,* X. 132.
auf, prep. gov. acc. or dat., *on, up*, upon, at,* IX. 99.
aufs, contract. of auf=das, *on the.*
auf das beste (aufs beste), adverbial form of superlative used absolutely, *in the best manner;* see p. 30.
auf=fangen (fing . . . auf, auf gefangen), *to intercept;* see note, p. 33.
auf=geben (gab . . . auf, auf= gegeben), *to give up*,* VIII. 15.
auf=gesprungen, p.p. of auf= springen*, *to gush forth; to start.*
auf=raffen, *to snatch up.*
aufrecht, adv., *upright*.*
auf=schauen, *to look up.*
auf=scheuchen, *to scare up,* X. 46 ; to be scared [fr. scheu, akin to—shy].
auf=springen, *to gush forth; to start.*
auf=stehen, lit. *to stand up ; to get up.*
auf=steigen (stieg . . . auf, auf gestiegen), *to mount.*
auf=stellen, lit. *to set up ; to serve,* X. 3.

VOCABULARY.

auf=wachen, to wake up*, to awake.
Aug(e), =n, n., eye*.
aus, prep. gov. dat., out* of, from, VIII. 1.
aus=gebrochen, p.p. of aus= brechen, to break out*.
aus=langen, in the sense of aus= holen, to fetch a blow, X. 79.
Aus=spruch, =(e)s, "=, m., lit. expression; maxim, XI. 29 [fr. aussprechen, to express].
aus=ziehen (zog : . . aus; aus= gezogen), to draw out.

B

Baier=land, =es, n., Baiern, Bavaria.
bai(e)risch, adj., Bavarian.
bald, adv., soon.
bald . . . bald, now . . . now; at one time . . . at another.
band, pret. of binden, to bind*; to gird, X. 57.
bang(e), adv., anxiously.
Banner, =s, =, n., banner*.
barg, pret. of bergen, to conceal; to hide.
Bart, =es, "=e, m., beard*, whiskers.
Bäu(e)rin, =nen, f., peasant woman [comp. Dutch boer].

bäumen, sich, to rear, III. 8 [fr. Baum, i.e. to stand erect like a tree].
beben, to tremble; to quiver.
Becher, =s, =, m., beaker*.
Bedacht, =es, m. intent; deliberation; mit gutem—, see note 47, p. 35.
befreit, p.p. of befreien, to free*; to release; to rescue.
begegnen, to meet.
begehren, to desire; to call for [akin to—yearn].
begrüßen, transit., to greet*.
bei, prep. gov. dat., by*; but mostly denoting place (not the instrument, as in Engl.), at; at the house of; among (Fr. chez), VII. 4; in the name of, IV. 9; by, X. 99.
beide, adj., both*, the two.
bekannt, adj., known, VIII. 55.
bereit, adj. or adv., ready, prepared.
Berg, =es, =e, m., mountain, VII. 1 [compare—iceberg*].
Berglied, =es, =er, n., mountain-song, VII.
bergen (barg, geborgen; birg), to hide; to conceal [akin to —harbour].

berühmen, ſich), unusual for ſich rühmen, *to boast*, IX. 70.

beſah, pret. of beſehen, *to examine*.

beſann, pret. of beſinnen, *to consider*.

Beſcheid trinken, with dat. of pers., *to pledge one*.

beſprengen, *to (be)sprinkle*.

beſſer, adj. or adv., comparat. of gut, *better**.

beſteigen (beſtieg, beſtiegen), *to mount; to ascend*.

beſtieg, pret. of beſteigen, *to mount*.

beſtellen, *to order*.

Bett, =es, =en, n., *bed*, couch*.

Bettel=ſtab, =es, "=e, m., *beggar's staff*.

Bettler, =s, =, m. [fr. betteln, to beg alms], *beggar*.

Bettler=Königin, f., lit. *beggar-queen*.

Bettler=ſchaar, =en, f., *crowd of beggars*.

beugen, *to bend; to weigh down;* reflex. *to bow**.

bezwingen (bezwang, bezwun=gen), *to overcome; to conquer*.

bezwungen, p.p. of bezwingen, *to overcome; to conquer*.

Bier, =es, n., *beer**.

bin, first p. sing. pres. ind. of ſein, *to be**.

Birſch, f. [fr. bürſchen], *deer-stalking*.

bis, prep. or conj., lit. *as far as, up to*, II. 20.

bis, advl. conj., *until, till*.

bitten (bat, gebeten) um, *to beg, ask*.

bitter, adj. or adv., *bitter**.

blank, adj. or adv., *bright*, III. 5 [akin to—to blink] ; (fr. blank comes the Fr. blanc, and fr. the latter comes the Engl. blanch, blank).

blau, adj., *blue*;* hence—

Blaue, das, *blue sky*.

bleiben (blieb, geblieben), *to remain*.

bleich, adj., *pale*.

blicken, *to look*, VIII. 26 [akin to—blink].

blieb, pret. of bleiben, *to remain*.

blind, adj., *blind*.

Blitz, =es, =e, m., *lightning*, VII. 16 [akin to—blink].

Blitzen, n., infinit. used subst., *lightning, flashing*.

blitzen, *to lighten; to flash*, XIV. 35.

blühen, *to bloom* [akin to—to blow ; Lat. florēre].

blüten=reich, adj., lit. rich in blossoms; *flowery.*
Blut, =es, n., *blood*.*
Blut=ſtrahl, m., *jet, stream, of blood.*
Boden, =s, =, m., *bottom*, ground;* zu —, *down,* X. 98.
Bord, =es, =e, m. or n., *border*, brim.*
brach, pret. of brechen, *to break*.*
Brand, =es, "=e, m., *fire* [cp. firebrand*].
brannte, pret. of brennen, *to blaze,* X. 198; *to be kindled with,* XII. 43.
Brauch, =es, "=e, m., *usage, custom.*
brauſen, to roar; *to rush with a roar,* VII. 8.
brechen (brach, gebrochen, bricht), *to break*;* reflex. *to spend one's self,* XI. 56.
breit, adj. or adv., *broad*.*
brennen (brannte, gebrannt), *to burn*;* *to fire at.*
bricht, third pers. sing. pres. indicat. of brechen, *to break; to pluck.*
Brot (more correct than Brod), =es, =e, n., *bread*.*
Brück(e), =(e)n, f., *bridge*.*
Bruder, =s, "=, m., *brother*.*

Brunnen, =s, =, m., *fountain, well* [akin to—bourne].
Bruſt, "=e, f., *breast*, bosom,* XII. 32.
Burg, =en, f., *castle,* V. 2 [akin to—burgh, borough; cp. also bergen].
Buſch, =es, "=e, m., *bush*, thicket, brushwood.*

C

Chriſten=ſchaar, =en, f., *troops of Christians.*

D

da, adv., *there*, then.*
da, conj., *as, since.* As adverbs attract the verb, whilst conjunctions throw it to the end, it is easy to see, by the place of the verb, whether da is used as adv. or conj.
dabei, adv., *at the same time,* XIII. 16.
daher=kommen, *to come*. along.*
daher=ſprengen, lit. to gallop on; *to sweep along,* VIII. 19.
dahin=ſchwinden, *to vanish; to forsake.*
Dam(e), =en, f., *dame*, lady.*
Dänemark, n., *Denmark*.*
Dank, =es, m., *thanks** [akin to

denken, to think]; zu Dank, to satisfaction, XII. 33; to your heart's content.

dann, adv., then*.

darauf, adv. (comp. of auf + da(r), inverted), thereupon*.

darf, first or third p. sing. indic. of dürfen, to be allowed.

darob, adv. (comp. of ob + da(r), inverted), lit. thereover; i.e. through it.

daß, conj., that*.

dauern, to last [like Engl. to dure, and Fr. durer, fr. Lat. durare].

davon, adv. (comp. of von + da, inverted), lit. from there, thence, off and away, off, XI. 19; of which, X. 45; from which, XII. 46.

dazu, adv., moreover; nor, cp. note, p. 41.

dazwischen, adv., between*.

decken, to cover, to protect [akin to Lat. tegere].

Degen, =s, =, m., champion [akin to—thane]; (Degen, sword, is of different origin).

dem, dat. sing. of pers. pr., der.

denen, dat. pl. of der, demonstr. or pers. pr., to them.

denken (dachte, gedacht), to think*.

denn, adv., then*; conj., for.

der—(1) def. art. the; (2) pers. pr. he; (3) demonstr. pr. this; or (4) relat. pr. who.

dereinst, adv., some day.

derweil, obsolete, adv. conj., whilst, while*.

deß or deſſen, pers. demonstr., and relat. pr., whose, VIII. 13; his, X. 178, IX. 4 (used like Latin ejus).

deutsch, adj. or adv., German [fr. Old Germ. diot, folk, people; hence, through Lat., teuton, teutonic; cp. also Dutch with the restricted meaning of Low Dutch].

dicht, adj. or adv., dense [akin to—tight].

dienen, with dat. of pers., to serve, to wait on.

Diener, =s, =, m. (fr. dienen, to serve), servant.

Dienst, =es, =e, m., service.

dies, contr. of dieses, this*.

dir, pers. pr., dat. of du, to thee*.

doch, yet, however, IV. 3 [akin to—though].

Donner, =s, =, m., thunder.

VOCABULARY.

Donner=hall, =es, m. (unusual), clap of thunder.
dort, adv., there [akin to—da(r), there].
Drache, =n, =n, m., dragon*.
drauf, contract. of darauf (comp. of auf + da(r), transposed like its Engl. equivalent), thereupon*.
draus (comp. of da(r) + aus), out* of which.
draußen, adv. (comp. of dar + außen), outside, out* of doors.
drei, three*.
drein, adv., contract. of darein, into* it.
drein=blicken, lit. to look at (into) it ; to shed its light.
drin, adv., contract. of darin, therein.
dringen (drang, gedrungen), to burst forth, XIII. 38.
dritte, ord. numb., third*.
drüben, adv., over there, yonder.
Druck, =es, m., pressure, weight, X. 166.
drücken, to press ; to squeeze.
drum, adv., contract. of darum, there-*fore.
duftig, adj. or adv. [fr. Duft], fragrant.
dumpf, adj. or adv., hollow [akin to—damp].

dunkel, adj. or adv., dark, dusky, III. 3.
durch, prep. gov. acc., through*.
durch=beben, to thrill ; to send a thrill.
durchdringen, insep. (durch=drang, durchdrungen), to penetrate ; to pervade.
dürsten, to be thirsty.

E

eben, adj., even*.
eben, adv., just, VI. 12.
edel, adj. or adv., noble [akin to O. E. athel].
Edel=stein, =(e)s, =e, m., precious (lit. noble) stone, gem, X. 6.
eh' (ehe), adv., ere* ; i.e. before.
Ehr(e), =n, f., honour.
ehren=voll, adj., honourable.
Eiche, =n, f., oak*.
eigen, adj., own*.
Eigentum, =s, "=er, n., ownership, property.
Eiland, =es, =e, n., island* ; see note, p. 49.
eilen, to hasten ; to hurry ; to make speed.
Eil(e), f., hurry, haste.
Ein=er, =e, =es, subst. form of ein, one*, VII. 27.
eingekehret, p.p. of einkehren,

lit. to turn in; here (II.) to put up.

Einkehr, f. [fr. einkehren, lit. to turn in], putting up at an inn.

ein=mal, adv., once, one day, once upon a time [mal, akin to Engl. meal, in piece-meal].

Eins, n., numeral used as subst., one* (thing).

Einsamkeit, f., solitude, IX. 28.

ein=schenken, trans., to pour out into the cup; to fill the glasses with.

ein=setzen, to set*, X. 194.

einst, adv., once, one* day, VII. 21.

ein=stürmen, to rush in.

Eisen, =s, =, n., iron*, V. 11.

Eisenstang(e), =(e)n, f., iron bar; see note, p. 32.

eitel, adj. or adv., vain [akin to—idle].

entgelten (entgalt, entgolten) lassen, to requite.

entrissen, p.p. of entreißen, to snatch away; to wrest.

entrollen, to roll away; to fall down.

entstellt, p.p. of entstellen, to disfigure; to deface.

Erde, =en, f., earth*, ground.

Erd(en)=ball, =es, m., terrestrial ball (globe).

erdröhnen, to roar.

erdrücken, to crush.

erfand, pret. of erfinden, to invent; to find, p. 31.

erfinden (erfand, erfunden), lit. to invent; to find; see p. 31.

erfreuen, to rejoice; to regale.

ergreifen (ergriff, ergriffen), to seize.

erheben (erhob, erhoben), to raise; to exalt; to elevate; reflex. to arise, XV. 45.

erhoben, p.p. of erheben, to arise; to raise.

erjagen, to catch; to kill; see note, p. 29.

erklang, pret. of erklingen, to resound.

erlag, pret. of erliegen, to succumb.

erschallen (erscholl, erschollen, or regular), to resound.

erschauen, to descry.

erschlug, pret. of erschlagen, to slay*.

erscholl, pret. of erschallen, to resound.

erst, ord. numb., first*; da erst, then only, VIII. 34; am ersten; see note, p. 33.

erſtieg, pret. of erſteigen, to scale.
erſtochen, p.p. of erſtechen, insep. comp. v., to pierce; to stab, III. 1.
erwecken, to awaken*; to rouse.
Erz=biſchof, =(e)s, "=e, m., arch-bishop*.
es (contract. 's), n. pers. pr., it*, there; see note, p. 29.
euch, pers. pr., acc. or dat. of ihr, to you.
ewig, adj., eternal, VI. 14; adv. for evermore, X. 140 [akin to Lat. ævum].

F

fachen, to fan; to stir.
fahr(e)wol, farewell*.
Fall, =es, "=e, m., fall*; zu Fall bringen, to fell, VIII. 33. zum Fall kommen, to come to grief.
fallen (fiel, gefallen), to fall*.
fand(en), pret. of finden, to find*.
fangen (fing, gefangen), to catch [akin to fang, hence — finger].
Fant, stripling [akin to infant].
Farbe, =n, f., colour.
faſſen, to seize, VIII. 34.
faſt, adv., almost, nearly, VIII. 10.

fechten (fochten, gefochten), to fight*.
Fechter (from fechten), =s, =, m., fighter*, champion.
fehlen, with dat. of pers., to be missing; to be wanting; X. 11 [akin to—to fail].
Fei, Fee, =n, f., fay, fairy, [from Fr. fée, Lat. fatum.]
feiern, to rest on one's oars; to make holiday.
fein, adj. or adv., fine*, noble, IX. 36.
Feind, =es, =e, m., enemy [akin to—fiend].
Feld, =es, =er, n., field*.
Fell, =es, =e, n., skin, hide; see note, p. 30.
Fels, =en(=ens), =en, m., rock.
Felſen=kluft, "=e, f., lit. rocky cleft.
Felſen=wand, "=e, f., rocky wall.
Fels=verließ, =es, =e, n., rocky cave, cavern; see note, p. 49.
fern(e), adj. or adv., far*, far off, X. 176.
Fern(e), f., distance.
feſt, adj. or adv., strong, firm, XI. 55 [akin to—fast].
Feſt=trommeten=ſchall, m., festive trumpet-call (clangour).

VOCABULARY.

euer, =ě, =, n., *fire**.
el, pret. of fallen, *to fall**.
nben (fand, gefunden), *to find**.
ng... an, pret. of anfangen, *to begin*.
nster, adj. or adv., *dark, dusky*.
ifdj, =eš, =e, m., *fish**.
lamme, =n, f., *flame**; Flammen schlagen, *to blaze*, V. 12.
leiß, =eš, m., *industry, diligence*, V. 15 [akin to fließen, *to flow*].
ink, adj. or adv., *briskly, deftly, nimbly*.
oh, pret. of fliehen, *to flee*.
löte, =n, f., *flute**.
lud), =eš, "=e, m., *curse*, XIV.
lut, =en, f., *torrent** [akin to —flood].
rdjt, old provincial pret. of fürchten, *to fear*, VIII. 23 [akin to—fright].
:agen, *to ask; to inquire* (cp. Lat. rogare).
:ank, adj. or adv., *free*, XII. 34; *boldly*, III. 6.
rau, =en, f., *woman, wife, Mrs.*
rauen=bild, =eš, =er, n.; see note, p. 37.
räulein, =š, n., dim. of Frau, *young lady, her ladyship*.

frei, adj. or adv., *free*, open*,
IX. 3; *freely, merrily, blithe*, IX. 79.
Freiheit, =en, f., *freedom, liberty*.
fressen (fraß, gefressen, friß), *to devour*.
freuden=voll, adj., *full of joy, overjoyed*.
freudig, adj. or adv., *joyful, merry*, XIII. 22.
freu(e)n sich, an, *to rejoice at; to delight in*; (sich freuen... auf, *to rejoice by anticipation*).
frisch, adj. or adv., *fresh*, brisk**, XI. 45; *briskly*, XIV. 12.
froh, adj. or adv., *glad, cheerful*.
fromm, adj. or adv., *godly, pious*.
Fug, =eš, m., *right*; mit —, *rightly, deservedly*.
fühlen, *to feel**.
fuhr, pret. of fahren, *to cross; to sail*.
führen, *to lead; to conduct; to carry on; to deal*, XII. 45, 47.
fünfzig, *fifty*.
furchtbar=prächtig, adj., lit. *fiercely splendid*, i.e. *in awe-inspiring splendour*.

Fürſt, =en, =en, m., *prince* [akin to—first; cp. Lat. princeps, lit. taking the first place; Fr. and Engl. prince].

Fuß, =es, ̈=e, m., *foot**; zu Fuß, *on foot*, X. 169.

G

Gab(e), =n, f. [from geben], *gift*.

gab, pret. of geben, *to give; to yield*, X. 195.

ganz, adj. or adv., *whole*, VIII. 55.

gar, adv., *very, so very*, X. 142, 168 [akin to—*yare* = ready].

Garten, =s, ̈=, m., *garden**.

Gaſt, =es, ̈=e, m., *guest**; zu Gäſte ſein; see note, p. 30.

Ge=, collective prefix. Nouns compounded with Ge= are as a rule *masc.*, if ending in a verbal stem; *neuter*, if ending in =e (expressed or dropped)—der Geſang; das Gefild(e).

Gebein, =es, =e, n. (comp. of collect. pref. ge + bein), *bones**.

geben (gab, gegeben), *to give**.

Gebirg(e), =s, =, n., *mountain-range* (comp. of collective prefix ge + berg).

geborſten, p.p. of berſten, *to burst**.

gebracht, p.p. of bringen, *to bring**.

gebrochen, p.p. of brechen, *to break**.

gedacht(e), pret. of gedenken, *to remember; to intend; to think*, X. 50; see note, p. 39.

Gedräng(e), =s, n., *crowd, press, throng**, IX. 33.

gefallen laſſen, es ſich (dat.), *to put up with; to submit to*.

Gefilde, =s, =, n., *fields* (comp. of the collect. pref. ge + feld).

geflogen, p.p. of fliegen, *to fly**, VI. 6.

Gehege, =s, =, n., *copse*, X. 39; see note, p. 39 [akin to—hedge].

geholfen, p.p. of helfen, *to help**.

Geiſt, =es, =er, m., *ghost, spirit, demon*, XI. 26.

Geißel, =n, f., *scourge*.

Geklaff, =es, n., collect. n. [fr. klaffen], *yelping, barking*; see note, p. 29.

gelehnt, p.p. of lehnen, *to lean**; *leaning, propped*; see note, p. 49.

gellen, lit. *to yell**; gellend, *ringing*.

gellen, intrans., *to yell; to resound*.

gelten (galt, gegolten), with dat. of pers., *to be aimed at; to be meant for*, VI. 7.

Gemahl, =ẽ, =e, m., *consort, husband*, IX. 9.

Gemahl, n.; see note, p. 47.

Genoß(e), =n, =n, m., *companion*, XIV. 12 [fr. genoß, pret. of genießen].

genug, adv., *enough*.

geritten, p.p. reiten, *to ride**.

gern, adv., *fain* [akin to—*to yearn*]; ich wäre gern, *I would fain be*, i.e. *I should like to be;* gern(e) singen, *to be fond of singing*.

Geroll, =es, n., *rumbling*.

gerufen, p.p. of rufen, *to call*.

Gesang, =es, "=e, m., *song**, *singing**.

geschehe(e)n, *to happen*; see note, p. 36.

Geschlecht, =es, =er, n., *race, kith and kin*, IX. 108.

Geschrei, =es, =e, n. (comp. of collect. pref. ge + schrei, shriek), *shouts*.

geschwind, adj. or adv., *quick, quickly*, IX. 15.

geschwungen, p.p. of schwingen, *to swing**.

gesehn, p.p. of sehen, *to see**.

Gesell, =en, =en, m., *companion, apprentice*, V. 14.

gesprochen, p.p. of sprechen, *to speak**.

gestritten, p.p. of streiten, *to fight*.

gesund, adj. or adv., *sound*, healthy; hale, hearty*, X. 143.

gesungen, p.p. of singen, *to sing**.

getaucht, p.p. of tauchen, *to plunge; to steep* [akin to—*to duck*].

gethan, p.p. of thun, *to do**.

gewaltig, adj or adv., *mighty, powerful, formidable*.

Gewand, =(e)s, "=er, n., *garment*.

gewandt, p.p. of wenden, *to turn round*.

gewesen, p.p. of sein, *to be*.

Gewölb(e), =es, =, n., *vault*.

Gezelt, =es, =e, n., *tent* [Zelt is akin to—*tilt*].

gezogen, pret. of ziehen, *to march;* see note, pp. 32 and 33.

gi(e)b, second pers. sing. imperat. of geben, *to give**.

giebt, third pers. sing. pres. indic. of geben, *to give**.

gießen (goß, gegoſſen), *to pour* [akin to—gush].

gilt, third pers. sing. pres. indic. of gelten, *the question is;* see note, p. 47.

gingen, pret. of gehen, p.p. gegangen, *to go**.

Gipfel, =s, =, m., *top, summit*.

Glanz, =es, m., *glitter, gleam, glare*.

glänzen [fr. glanz], *to shine; to glitter*.

Glas, =es, "=er, n., *glass**.

glauben, with dat. of person, *to believe*.

gleich, adj. gov. dat., *like, equal*.

gleich, ſogleich, adv., *at once*.

Glied, =es, =er, n., *member, limb, joint; rank,* VII. 23; see note, p. 33.

Glück, =es, =e, n., *luck**, XIII.; *good luck, happiness*.

Glut, =en, f., *glow**.

gnädig, adj. or adv., *graciously*.

Gold, =es, n., *gold**.

golden [fr. Gold], adj., *golden**.

Gold=geſchirr, n., *gold-plate;* see note, p. 38.

Gold=pokal, m., *gold-goblet*.

Gott, =es, "=er, m., *God**.

Gottes=ſtreiter, =s, =, m., lit. *God's champions*.

Grab, =es, "=er, n., *grave**.

Grab=gesang, m., *dirge*.

Graf, =en, =en, m., *earl, count*.

grau, adj. or adv., *gray*.

graus, adj. or adv., *horrid, hideous*.

Graus, =es, m., *horror* [akin to—grue* in gruesome].

greifen (griff, gegriffen), *to seize* [akin to—grip].

Greis, =es, m., *old man* [fr. adj. greis, gray, grizzled*].

griff, pret. of greifen, *to seize*.

Grimm, =es, m., *wrath* [akin to—grim].

grob, adj. or adv., *coarse, rude* [akin to—gruff].

groß, adj. or adv., *great*, big, large, tall*.

grün, adj. or adv., *green**.

Grund, =es, "=e, m., *ground**.

gülden, old form of golden, *gold(en)**, adj.

gut, adj. or adv., *good*, well*.

Gut(e), =s, n., subst. form of gut, *good**; see note, p. 37.

H

Haar, =es, =e, n., *hair**.

Hag=es, "=e, m., *copse* [akin to—hedge*].

Hain, =es, =e, m., *grove.*
halb, adj. or adv., *half.*
Halle, =n, f., *hall*.*
halt, adv., indeed, *you see.*
halten (hielt, gehalten), *to hold*;
  to stop.*
Hammer, =s, "=, m., *hammer*.*
Hand, "=e, f., *hand.*
Hände=zittern, n., lit. *trembling
  of hands.*
Harfe, =n, f., *harp*.*
Harm, =es, m., *grief, despair,*
  XV. 5 [akin to—harm*].
Harnisch, =es, =e, m., *harness*,
  armour.*
harren, *to tarry.*
Hast, f., *haste*, hurry.*
hatte(n), pret. of haben, *to
  have*.*
hauen (hieb, gehauen), *to hew*,
  to cut.*
Haupt, =es, "=er, n., *head*.*
Haus, =es, "=er, n., *house*.*
heben, *to lift;* reflex. *to rise*
  [akin to—to heave].
Heer, =es, =e, n., *army, host.*
Heeres=zug, =es, "=e, m., lit.
  *train (march) of army;
  expedition,* VIII. 18.
hehr (old comparat. of hoch),
  lofty, august, IX. 5 ; see
  note, p. 46.
bei! interj., *hey!*

heida! interj., *stop!*
Heide=land, =es, n., *heath* [fr.
  die Heide (Haide) is derived
  der Heide; as in English
  heathen from *heath;* cp.
  also the French païen, from
  Lat. paganus, fr. pagus].
Heil, =es, =e, n., *welfare, pros-
  perity,* IX. 135 [akin to—
  hale, whole, healthy].
heil! interj., *hail!*
Heiland, =s, =e, m., *Saviour*
  [O. G. part. pres. of heilen].
heilig, adj., *holy*, saint,*
  VIII. 2.
Heiligkeit, f., *holiness*.*
heißen (hieß, geheißen), *to bid;
  to be called* [akin to—to
  hight, obsol.]
Held, =en, =en, m., *hero.*
Heldenbild, =es, =er, n. [fr.
  Held, hero], *heroic figure.*
Helden=buch, n., lit. *book*
  (chronicle) *of heroes.*
helfen (half, geholfen), *to help*;
  to avail,* XI. 11
hell, adj. or adv., *bright, clear,
  loud, clean,* X. 109 ;
  blithely, XII. 12.
Helle, f., *brightness.*
her, adv., *hither;* see note, p.
  45 ; adv. expletive added
  to prepositions, *along,* p. 39.

herab, adv. (comp. of her + ab), *down*, V. 2.

herab=sehen, *to look down upon.*

herauf=blicken, *to look up.*

heraus (her + aus), *out hither, forth :* in contradistinction to hin=aus, *out hence, out of,* VII. 7.

herein=brechen (brach .. herein, herein=gebrochen), lit. break in, *to charge.*

herein=führen, *to introduce.*

herein=kommen (kam ... herein, herein=gekommen), *to come in.*

herein=treten (trat ... herein, herein=getreten), *to step in.*

herfür=drücken, sich, *to press forward;* see note, p. 36.

hernach, *afterward.*

Herr, =n, =en, m., *lord, sir, master,* III. 1.

herrlich, adj. or adv., lit. *lordly, glorious, delightfully,* XII. 39.

herum, *round about, around,* VII. 12.

herum=zieh(e)n, *to gather round.*

herunter=hauen, *to (cut) hew* *down.*

herunter=sinken (sank ... her= unter, herunter=gesunken), *to sink* *(fall) down.*

Herz, =ens, =en, n., *heart*.*

Herzog, =(e)s, "=e, m., *duke** [comp. of Heer + zog, pret. of ziehen, akin to—Engl. tug, Lat. ducere].

heulen, *to howl*.*

heut(e), adv., *to-day* [formed exactly like the Lat. hodie (hoc + die), fr. old demonstr. hiu + tag].

heutig, adj., formed fr. heute, *to-day's ; this,* XII. 35 (in am heutigen Tag, the word *day* is contained twice —on this day's day, as in the French—aujourd'hui [hui, from Lat. hodie]).

hieb, pret. of hauen, *to hew; to cut.*

Hieb, =es, =e, m. [fr. pret. of hauen, *i.e.* hieb], *thrust.*

hielt(en), pret. of halten, *to hold*.*

hier, adv., *here*.*

hieß(en), pret. of heißen, *to bid; to order,* X. 20.

hilf, second p. sing. imperat. of helfen, *to help*.*

Himmel, =s, =, m., *heaven,* IX. 106 ; *sky.*

himmlisch, adj. or adv., *heavenly.*

hinab, adv. (comp. of hin, *thither,* + ab, *down*), *down,* III. 10 ; *downwards.*

hinab=gehen (ging ... hinab, hinab = gegangen), to go* down.

hinab=rufen, to call down.

hinaus, adv. (comp. of hin + aus), forth, V. 4.

hinaus=wandern, to wander*, to roam, to rove.

hindurch=schneiden (schnitt ... hindurch, hindurch = ge = schnitten), to cut (cleave) right through, VIII. 44.

hinein=sprengen, to charge.

hinter, prep. gov. dat. or acc., behind*; hinter, her, behind, X. 33.

hinterm, contract. of hinter and dem.

hin=treten, to step forth.

hinunter=laufen, to run down.

Hirsch, =es, =e, m., stag, hart*.

Hirtenknab(e), =(e)n, m. (comp. of Hirt, herdsman* + knabe, boy), shepherd boy, VII. 1.

hoch, adj. or adv., high, IV. 12; tall, XII. 18, 38.

Hof, =es, "=e, m., court, IX. 94; court-yard, XII. 6, IX. 29.

Hof=gesind, =es, n., lit. court-attendance, servants.

Höflings=schar, =en, f., train of courtiers.

hoh(em), see hoch; das Hohe, what is exalted; the sublime.

Höhe, =n, contracted Höhn, f., hill, height*.

höhen [fr. hoch], to heighten* ; to raise.

hold, adj. or adv., lovely.

holen, to fetch.

Hölle, =n, f., hell*.

horchen, to hearken*; to listen.

hören, to hear*.

Hörer, =s, =, m., lit. hearer*, listener.

Horn, =es, "=er, n., horn*.

Hort, =es, =e, m., charm, palladium [akin to—hoard].

hub(en), old pret. of heben; see anheben.

Hund, =es, =e, m., hound*, dog.

Hünen=schwert, =es, =er, n. ; lit. giant's sword; see note, p. 49.

husch, interj.; see note, p. 29.

I

ihm (pers. pr. dat. sing. m. of er), to him*; see note, p. 29; see also note to mir, p. 32.

ihn, pers. pr. act. of er, him*.

im, contr. of in=dem (dat.), in the.

immer, adv., *always, ever;* noch —, *still,* X. 11.

inmitten, prep. gov. gen., *in the midst* of.*

ins, contr. of in=das, *into the.*

irren, *to wander* [akin to—Lat. errare, to err].

J

ja, adv., *yes, aye, indeed.*

jagen, lit. to chase; to hunt; *to roll; to swell; to surge,* XI. 12.

Jäger, =s, =, m., *hunter, huntsman, sportsman;* from jagen, Jagd; see note, p. 29.

jäh, adj. or adv., *sudden,* steep.

Jährlein, =s,=, n., dim. of Jahr, *year.*

Jed=er, =e, =es, adj. or subst., *every one* [akin to—either].

jetzt, adv., *now* [akin to—yet].

jung, adj., *young*, youthful.*

Jüngling, =s, =e, m. (comp. of jung + dim. suffix—ling), stripling, *youth,* IV. 11.

jüngst, adv. derived fr. superl. of jung, *lately, recently, but a short time ago.*

K

Kaiser, =s, =, m., *emperor,* VIII. 1 [from Lat. Cæsar].

kalt, adj. or adv., *cold*.*

kam=en, pret. of kommen, *to come*.*

Kamerad, =en, =en, m., *comrade** [like the Engl. comrade, Fr. camarade; fr. Span. camarada; fr. Lat. camara].

Kampf=geschrei, n., battle-cries.

kämpfen, *to fight; to contend* [akin to—Lat. campus].

kann, first and third p. sing. pres. indic. of können, *to be able; can*,* VI. 13.

kaum, adv., *scarcely, hardly.*

keck, adj. or adv., *bold, saucy.*

kehren, to turn; *to return,* IX. 50.

Kein=er, =e, =es, indef. pron.-adj., used as substantive, *no one,* X. 4.

Kelch=glas, n., *glass or crystal goblet* [akin to—chalice, fr. Lat. calix].

kennen (kannte, gekannt), *to know;* in the sense of—connaître; cognosco.

Kind, =es, =er, n., *child* [akin to—kin, kind, etc.].

klagen, *to lament; to bewail.*

klang, pret. of klingen, *to sound; to ring.*

Klang, =es, "=e, m. [fr. pret. of

klingen], *sound, clang*, tune.*
klar, adj. or adv., *clear, bright,* X. 5.
Kleid, =eß, =er, m., *clothes*, garments.*
Kleinod, =ß, =e, or =ien, n., *gem, jewel,* X. 10.
Klinge, =n, f., *blade.*
klingen (klang, geklungen), *to ring; to sound.*
klirren, *to clatter; to clank.*
klopfen, *to beat;* to knock; to clap; see p. 29.
Kluft, "=e, f., lit. *cleft*, cave, cavern,* XV. 17.
Knabe, =n, =n, m., *boy, lad,* V. 1 [akin to—knave].
Knall, =eß, "=e, m., *clap, report.*
Knecht, =eß, =e, m., *squire,* III. 1; *servant,* XII. 9 [akin to —knight]; see p. 31.
Knie, =ß, =, n., *knee*.*
kommen (kam, gekommen), *to come*.*
kommen laſſen, *to send for,* VIII. 50.
König, =ß, =e, m., *king*.*
Königs=krone, =en, f., *king's (royal) crown.*
Königs=ſohn, =eß, "=e, m., *king's son*.*

Königs=wort, n., *kingly (royal) word*.*
Kopf, =eß, "=e, m., *head,* VIII. 35 [indir. fr. Lat. cuppa]. The originally Germ. word for, and akin to, *head* is Haupt, now used in poetic diction and compounds.
Koſt, f. [fr. koſten, to taste], *fare, food.*
koſten, *to cost*.*
köſtlich, adj. or adv., *costly*, delicious.*
Kraft, "=e, f., *strength, force,* IV. 11 [akin to—craft].
kräftig, adj. or adv., *strong, vigorous.*
krank, adj., *ill, sick.*
Kranz, =eß, "=e, m., *garland.*
Kreis, =eß, =e, m., *circle.*
Krieger, =ß, =, m., *warrior.*
Kron(e), =n, f., *crown** [fr. Lat. corona].
krumm, adj. or adv., *curved.*
Kryſtall, =eß, =e, m., *crystal*.*
Kugel, =n, f., *bullet, cannon-ball.*
kühl, adj. or adv., *cool.*
kühn, *bold* [akin to—keen].
Kunde, =n, f., *science, tidings, intelligence,* VIII.
künftig [fr. kommen], *future.*
kunnt, old form of konnte,

pret. of können, *can, to be able*, V. 17.
kurz, adj. or adv., *short* [akin to—curt, and to—short].

L

laben, *to refresh.*
lachen, *to laugh*.*
laden, *to load*.*
lag(en), pret. of liegen, *to lie*.*
Land, =es, "=er, n. (or Lande, poetical), *land*, country.*
lang, adj., *long*.*
lange, *long time*; nicht, *before long*, XII. 17.
langsam, adj. or adv., *slowly, at a slow pace.*
längst, *longest*,* VII. 3; am längsten; see note, p. 33.
Lanze, =n, f., *lance*.*
lassen (ließ, gelassen), *to let*;* *to allow*, V. 14; *to forsake; to renounce*, IX. 7.
Lauf, =es, "=e, m., *run, career*, VII. 8.
laufen (lief, gelaufen), *to run* [akin to—to leap].
lauschen, *to listen*, XV. 43; *to eavesdrop.*
laut, adj. or adv., *loud, aloud.*
läuten [fr. laut], *to ring.*
Leben, =s, n., *life.*

Lebenlang, mein, *all my life long.*
leer, adj. or adv., *barren*, VIII. 4; *empty.*
legen (lag, gelegen), *to lay; to place; to put*; reflex., *to lie down.*
lehren, *to reach.*
Leib, =es, =er, m., *body* [akin to —life].
Leiche, =n, f., *corpse* [akin to —lich, in lichgate].
Leichnam, =es, =e, m., *corpse.*
leicht, adj. or adv., *light*, IV. 6; *easy.*
leicht = beschwingt (comp. of leicht, *light*, + beschwingt, *winged*).
leid, adj. or adv., *painful;* used in impers. phrases —es ist (thut) mir leid, *I am sorry*, V. 8; see p. 32.
lenken, *to steer; to pilot.*
lenken . . . nach, intrans., *to wend one's way towards; to make for.*
Lenz, =es, m., poetical, *springtime* [akin to—lent].
letzt, adj., *last.*
leuchten, *to glitter.*
Leuchten, infinit. used as subst., n., *shining, gleaming.*

VOCABULARY. 71

licht, adj. or adv., *bright, dazzling.*

lieb, adj. or adv., *dear;* liebe Sonne, X. 196; see note, p. 42 [akin to—*love*].

lieb haben, *to hold dear.*

Lieb und Leid, alliteration, *in joy and sorrow; in good and evil days.*

Liebchen, =s, =, n. [der. fr. lieb, *love**], *sweetheart.*

Liebe, f., *love, affection.*

lieben, *to love*; *to be fond of.*

lieber, adv., compar. of lieb (*lief**), *rather.*

lieblich, adj. or adv., *lovely*.*

lief(en), pret. of laufen, *to run* [akin to—*to leap*].

liegen (lag, gelegen), *to lie*.*

ließ, pret. of lassen, *to let**; *to allow;* *to order.*

link, adj., *left.*

Linke, f., *left, left side* (hand); zur Linken, *to the left,* VIII. 39.

litt(en), pret. of leiden, *to suffer; to allow.*

Livrei, f., *livery*.*

lobesam, adj. (comp. of lob(e) + suffix sam, *some*), *praiseworthy.*

Locke, =n, f., *lock*.*

Lohn, =es, "=e, m., *reward, due.*

Loos, =es, =e, n., *lot*, fate;* zum Loos werden, with dat. of person, *to fall to the lot.*

los=machen, *to detach; to take off;* *to loosen,* X. 192.

Luft, "=e, f., *air* [akin to—*lift, loft*].

Lüftlein, =s, =, n., dim. of Luft, *breeze.*

Lust, "=e, f., *delight, treat,* XII. 23 [akin to—*lust*]; see note, p. 47.

lustig, adj. or adv. [fr. Lust], here *merrily, exultingly* [akin to—*lustily*].

lustig, adj., *brisk,* V. 12.

lustsam, adj., *unusual, for charming;* see note, p. 37.

M

machen, *to make,* V. 16; *to do,* VIII. 48.

Macht, "=e, f., *might.*

mächtig, adj. or adv. [from Macht], *mighty, huge,* X. 137.

Magen,=s,=, m., *stomach* [akin to—*maw.*]

Mahl, =es, =e, n., *meal, repast.*

Mähre, =n, f., *mare.*

Maien=licht, =es, n., *light of May.*

Mal, =es, =e, n., *time;* mit

einem —, *all at once*, IX.
105 [akin to — *meal*, in
piece-*meal*].
man, indef. pron., *one* [fr.
Mann, as the French *on*,
fr. Lat. homo].
manch, adj., *many a.*
mancherlei, adv., *of many kinds.*
Mannen, pl., m., retainers,
warriors, XII. 43.
Männer=würde, f., *manly worth.*
Mantel, =s, ":, m., mantle,
cloak.
Mark, =es, n., lit. marrow,
pith, *strength*; see note, p.
49.
Marmor=säule, =n, f., *marble
column.*
Maß, =es, =e, n., measure,
grasp, XI. 55.
Matte, =n, f., mat, *grassy plot*
[akin to—mead, meadow].
Mauer, =n, f., *wall.*
Meer, =es, =e, n., *sea* [akin to—
Lat. mare, and Engl. mere].
Meer(es)=arm, =es, =e, m., *frith.*
mehr, adv., comp. of viel,
more*.
mehr, adv., *more*; nicht —, *no
longer*, X. 131.
mein=en, *to mean**; *to think.*
Meister, =s, =, m., *master** [fr.
Lat. magister].

melden, *to mention*; *to record.*
Menge, =n, f., *crowd*, *throng*
[akin to—many].
Menschen = brust, f., *human
breast*.*
Menschen = herz, n., *human
heart*.*
mild(e), adj. or adv., *mild**,
gentle, *gently.*
mir, dat. of ich, *to me*; see
note, p. 29.
missen, *to miss*.*
mit, prep. gov. dat., *with* [akin
to—Gr. μετά].
Mittags=stund(e), f., *mid-day**,
noon.
Mitte, f., middle, X. 43; in
der — n; see note, p. 42.
möcht(e), pret. subj. of mögen,
may*.
Moder, =s, m., *mouldering.*
mögen (mochte, gemocht), *may*.*
Mond(en)=licht, =es, n., *moon-
light*.*
Mord, =es, =e, m., *murder**
(Mörder, murderer); mit
Mord und Brand verwüsten,
to waste with fire and
sword.
morgen, adv., *to-morrow*.*
Morgens, gen. used adverbially, *in the (of a) morning.*
Mund, =es, m., *mouth*.*

VOCABULARY. 73

munben, to taste; to smack; es
munbet mir, *I relish*, X. 168.
müſſen, mußte, gemußt, *must**,
to be obliged.
mußt(e), pret. of müſſen, *must,
to have to*, VIII. 2.
Mut, =es, m., *courage, spirits*,
XII. 72; der — ſchwindet mir,
my courage fails (quails)
me; in trübem —, *downcast*,
X. 148 [akin to—mood].
Mutter, "=, f., *mother**.
Mutter=haus, =es, "=er, n., lit.
motherhouse, i.e. *source,
fountainhead,* VII. 6.
Mutter=land, n., lit. *motherland*; see note, p. 38.

N

nach, prep. gov. dat., *after, for,
at*, VIII. 20.
nach=folgen, *to follow after.*
nach=laufen (lief ... nach, nach=
gelaufen), *to run after.*
nach=tragen (trug ... nach,
nach = getragen), *to carry
after.*
nach=ziehen, *to drag on.*
Nachen, =s, m., *skiff, boat.*
Nacht, "=e, f., *night**.
Nachtigall, =en, f., *nightingale**.
nahm, pret. of nehmen, *to take.*
nähren, *to nourish ; to feed ; to
treat* [cp. Lat. nutrire, Fr.
nourir, Eng. to nourish].
Name, =ns, =n, m., *name.*
'ne, for eine, *a*, VIII. 45, X.
135.
neben, prep. gov. acc. or dat.,
by the side of.
Necken, infin. used subst., n.,
to nettle ; to banter.
nein, adv., *no**.
'nen, for einen, XI. 45.
nennen (nannte, gennant), *to call.*
nicht, adv., *not* [akin to —
naught].
nicht mehr, adv., *no more, no
longer.*
nieber liegen, *to lie low*, i.e. *in
ruins.*
nieber=ſteigen, *to come down;
to descend.*
nieber=zwingen, *to force down.*
nimmer, adv., *never.*
nimmſt, nimmt, second and
third p. sing. pres. ind. of
nehmen, *to take.*
nit, in South Germ. dialect for
nicht, *not.*
noch, adv., *still* ; noch ſchnell
genug, *just in time*, X. 81;
nor, IV. 6.
noch, noch immer, adv., *still.*
Nord, =ens, or Norden, =s, m.,
north*.

VOCABULARY.

nordisch, adj., *northern*.
Nordlicht = schein, =s, m., *glare of northern light* (aurora borealis).
Normanne, =n, =n, m., *Norman*.*
Normannen=heer, n., *Norman host*.
Normannen = herzog, =s, m., *Duke of Normandy*.
nun, adv., *now*.*
nur, adv., *only*.

O

offen, adj. or adv., *open*.*
oft, adv., *often*.*
Ohm, Oheim, =s, =e, m., *uncle*; see note, p. 37.
ohn(e), prep. gov. acc., *without*.
Ohne=furcht, *fearless*; see note, p. 43.
Ohr, =es, =en, n., *ear*.*

P

packen, *to seize*.
Panier, =s, =e, n., *banner*.*
Panzer, =s, =, m., *coat of mail*.
Pfeil, =es, =e, m., *arrow, dart, shaft, bolt*, VIII. 25 [from Lat. pilum].
Pferd, =es, =e, n., *horse*, VIII. 9 [akin to—Engl. palfrey; see note to Roß, p. 31]; zu —, *on horseback*, XII. 12.

piff, paff; see p. 30.
Pilger=gewand, =es, "=er, n., *pilgrim's dress*.
plötzlich, adj. or adv., *sudden, suddenly, all at once*, VIII. 19.
Pokal, =es, =e, m., *cup, beaker*.
Pracht, f., *magnificence, pomp, high estate*, IX. 7.
Prall, =es, =e, m., *shock, rebound*.
Preis, =es, =e, m., *prize*, XIV. 42, XV. 38; *praise, honour*, XIII. 11.
Prunk = gemach, =es, "=er, n.; Prunk = saal, =es, "=e, m., *state-room*.
purpurn, adj. or adv., *purple*.*

Q

Quelle, f., or Quell, n., *source, well*,* X. 107.
Quer(e), f., *cross direction*; in die —, *athwart*.

R

Rache, f., *vengeance, revenge*; here, *retribution*, III.
Rache=geist, =es, =er, m., *avenging spirit*.
Rad, =es, "=er, n., *wheel* [akin to—Lat. rota].
rannte, pret. of rennen, *to run*.

VOCABULARY. 75

raften, *to rest*, V. 3.

Rat, =eß, m., pl. Ratſchläge (Räte = councillors), *advice, counsel.*

raten (riet, geraten), *to advise; to counsel.*

Räuber, =ß, =, m. [fr. rauben], *robber*.*

Raum, =eß, "=e, m., *room*, spacious hall.*

rauſchen, *to rush*; to rustle;* hence heraus = rauſchen, *to rush out.*

recht, adj. or adv., *right, well, aright,* X. 145 ; *right well,* XII. 10.

Rechte, f., *right, right side (hand);* zur Rechten, *to the right,* VIII. 39.

regen, *to stir.*

Regen=bogen, =ß, =, m., *rainbow*.*

Regenbogen=glanz, m., *rainbow tints.*

Reh, =eß, =e, n., *roe*, deer.*

reich, adj., *rich*.*

Reich, =eß, =e, n., *empire.*

reichen, *to stretch out,* VI. 11 ; *to reach*,* IX. 27.

Reihe, =n, f., *rank, line.*

reiten (ritt, geritten), *to ride*.*

Reitersmann, m., *i.e.* Reiter, VIII. 7.

Reliquien=ſtück, n., lit. *piece of relic*.*

rennen (rannte, gerannt), *to run.*

reuen, *to rue*; to repent;* eß reut mich, *I repent (it).*

Rhein, =(e)ß, m., *Rhine.*

rief, pret. of rufen, *to call.*

Rieſe, =n, =n, m., *giant.*

Rieſen=kleinod, n., *giant's gem.*

rieſen=ſtark, lit. *strong as giant.*

ringen (rang, gerungen), *to struggle,* III. 11 [akin to —*to wring*].

Ringen, =ß, n., *endeavours.*

rings, adv., *around,* VII. 12 [formed from Ring + adv. suffix =ß; thus Tags, Abends, etc.]

riet, pret. of raten, *to advise; to counsel.*

Riß, =eß, =e, m. [fr. riß, pret. of reißen], *rent, rift.*

ritt(en), pret. of reiten, *to ride*.*

Ritter, =ß, =, m., *knight* [akin to—Reiter, fr. reiten, *to ride*].*

Ritterſaal, =eß, "=e, m., lit. *knights-hall,* i.e. *banquethall,* IX. 22.

Ritterſchaft, =en, f. (comp. of Ritter, *knight,* + ſchaft, *ship*), *knighthood.*

Röcheln, =ß, n., *death-rattle.*

Rolands-Lied, n., Song of Roland, the chief Old French epic poem; composed in the eleventh century.

Rose, -n, f., rose*.

Roß, -es, -e, n., horse, steed, III. 6 [akin to—horse; see p. 31].

Rößlein, -s, -, n., dim. of Roß, pony, nag.

rot, adj. or adv., red*.

Roter, i.e. Rotwein, m., red wine*.

Rücken, -s, -, m., back [akin to—ridge; cp. Berg-rücken].

rudern, to row, III. 11 [akin to—rudder].

rufen (rief, gerufen), to call.

Ruh(e), f., rest, repose.

ruhig, adj. or adv., quiet, quietly, IX. 47.

Ruhm, -es, m., glory, fame.

rühren, to wield, XII. 32; to touch, XIV. 16.

Rumpf, -es, "-e, m., trunk [akin to—rump].

Rüstung, -en, f., armour, III. 5 [fr. rüsten, to fit out; to arm].

S

's, abbreviation of es, III. 10.

Saal, -es, pl. Säle, m., hall.

Säbel, -s, -, m., sabre*; krummer —, scimitar, VIII. 28.

sachte, adj. or adv., gently, quietly.

sagen, to say*.

sah, pret. of sehen (p.p. gesehen), to see.

Saite, -n, f., chord, string.

Saiten-spiel, -es, n., lit. chord-play, i.e. music of stringed instruments.

sammt, prep. gov. dat., together with.

Sand, -es, m., sand*.

sang(en), pret. of singen, to sing.

Sang, -es, "-e, m., song*.

Sänger, -s, -, m., minstrel.

Sänger-greis, m., hoary minstrel.

Sänger-paar, -es, -e, n., minstrel pair.

Sängertum, -es, n., minstrelsy.

saß(en), pret. of sitzen, to sit, IX. 1.

Sattel, -s, "-, m., saddle.

Sattel-knopf, -es, "-e, lit. saddle-knot, pommel, VIII. 36.

satteln, to saddle*.

Säule, -n, f., pillar, column.

Säulen-saal, -es, "-e, n., pillared hall.

sausen, to whiz; to whir.

Schaar, =en, f., *troop, host.*
Schall, =es, "=e, m., *sound, report, clank.*
Schande, f., *shame, disgrace, infamy.*
scharf, adj. or adv., *sharp*.*
Schatten, =s, =, m., *shade*, shadow.**
schauen, *to look.*
Schaum, =es, "=e, m., *froth* [akin to—scum]; see note, p. 36.
schäumen, *to foam.*
schau(e)rig, schauerlich, adj. or adv., *awfully.*
Schein, =es, =e, m., *light, lustre,* [akin to—sheen].
Schenk, =es, =e [fr. Mund=schenk], *cup-bearer,* IX. 74.
Scherbe, =n, f., *fragment* [akin to—scarf, sherd].
scheu, adj. or adv., *shy.*
schier, adv., South Germ. for fast, beinahe, *well-nigh, almost, nearly.*
schießen (schoß, geschossen), *to shoot*.*
Schiff, =es, =e, n., *ship*, boat;* zu — e, *on board a ship,* XI. 32.
Schild, =es, =e, m., *shield;* hence Schild, =es, =er, n., *signboard,* II. 3, because signboards had the form of a shield.

Schild=träger, =s, =, m., *shield-bearer.*
Schilder=klang, m., *clanging of shields.*
Schimmer, =s, =, m., *lustre,* X. 9 [akin to—shimmer*].
schirmen, *to defend; to protect; to fence* [akin to—screen].
Schlaf, =es, m., *sleep*.*
schlafen (schlief, geschlafen), *to sleep*.*
Schlag, =es, "=e, m., *blow, thrust.*
schlagen (schlug, geschlagen), *to strike; to beat; to slay*;* die Harfe —, *play* (lit. *to strike) the harp;* um=schlagen, trans. *to wrap round.*
schlägt, third pers. sing., pres. indic. of schlagen.
schleudern, *to hurl; to throw.*
schlimm, adj. or adv., *treacherous,* XI. 17.
Schloß, =es, "=er, n., *castle.*
Schluck, =es, "=e, m., *draught, sip.*
schlug, pret. of schlagen, *to beat, to strike* [akin to—to slay].
schlürfen, *to sip.*
Schmaus, =es, "=e, m., *feast, treat.*
Schmerz, =e(n)s, =en, m., *pain, grief* [akin to—smart].

schmettern, *to sound.*
Schmied, =es, =e, m., *smith*, blacksmith.*
Schmiede, =n, f., *smithy* [fr. schmieden].
schmieden, *to forge,* V. 32 [akin to—smite].
schmuck, adj. or adv., *smart, stately,* XIV. 11.
schnell, adj. or adv., *quick, quickly.*
schon, adv., *already.*
schöpfen, *to draw* [akin to—shape].
schoß, pret. of schießen, intrans. *to fall; to be hurled.*
Schrecken, =s, =, m., *fright, scare, terror,* XIV. 7.
schrecklich, adj. or adv., *fiercely.*
schreiben (schrieb, geschrieben), *to write* [akin to—Lat. scribere].
schreien (schrie, geschrien), *to cry; to exclaim.*
schrieb, pret. of schreiben, *to write.*
Schritt, =es, =e, m., *step, pace, stride* [from schreiten, *to stride*].
Schuldigkeit, =en [fr. schuldig + suffix =keit], lit. *indebtedness;* here *score, bill, reckoning.*

schüren, *to poke; to rake.*
Schüssel, =n, f., *dish.*
Schutt, =es, m., *ruins, débris.*
schütteln, *to shake.*
Schwabe, =n, =n, m., *Suabian*.*
Schwaben=land, n., *Suabia*.*
Schwabenstreich, =es, =e, m.; see note, p. 35.
schwäbisch, adj., *Suabian.*
schwach, adj. or adv., *weak.*
Schwall, =es, "=e, m., lit. *swell*, revelry.*
schwand, pret. of schwinden, *to vanish; to fail.*
schwang, pret. of schwingen, *to swing*.*
Schwang, =es, m., from pret. of schwingen, VIII. 54; see note, p. 35.
Schwarm, =es, "=e, m., lit. *swarm*, crowd, throng.*
schweifen, *to roam; to range* [akin to—sweep].
schweigen (schwieg, geschwiegen), *to be silent; to be hushed.*
schwenken, *to wheel (about).*
schwer, adj. or adv., *heavy,* III. 12 [akin to—sore].
Schwere, adj. used substantively, *strait, pass, difficulty.*
Schwert, =es, =er, n., *sword*.*
Schwerter=schlag, =s, m., *clank, clashing of swords.*

VOCABULARY.

Schwester, =n, f., *sister**.
schwingen (schwang, geschwung-
 en), *to swing**, IV. 12 ; reflex. *to waft ; to take wings.*
schwitzen, *to sweat** ; *to perspire.*
schwoll, pret. of schwellen, *to
 swell** ; to heave.*
Sclaven-schritt, m., *tread of
 slaves**.
sechs, *six**.
segnen, *to bless.*
sehen (sah, gesehen, sieh), *to see ;
 to look,* IX. 57.
sehen . . . am, *to see by ;* see
 note, p. 36.
sehr, adv., *very, very much,
 sorely**, XI. 21.
seiden, adj., *silk(en).*
sein, seine, sein, poss. adj., *his.*
sein (war, gewesen), *to be.*
Seite, =n, f., *side ;* auf die
 Seite, *aside,* X. 81.
selber, adv., *self, himself,* III. 2.
selbst, *self, himself ;* see p. 30.
selig, adj. or adv., *blessed,
 blissful,* XIV. 25.
seltsam, adj. or adv. (comp. of
 selten, *seldom,* + sam, suff.
 -some), *strange, wondrous.*
senken, *to cast down,* IX. 117 ;
 to cast down ; to hang, X.
 186 ; *to lower,* X. 149.

sinken (sank, gesunken), *to sink.*
setzen, *to set ; to place.*
seufzen, *to sigh.*
Seufzer, =s, =, m., *sigh.*
sich, refl. pron. third p., m. f.
 and n., sing. and pl., *himself, herself, itself, one's self,
 themselves.*
Sieg, =es, =e, m., *victory.*
sieht, third p. sing. pres. ind.
 of sehen, *to see**.
singen (sang, gesungen), *to sing.*
Sinn, =es, =e, m., *mind, sense.*
sinnen, *to meditate.*
Skalde, =n, =n, m., *bard ;* see
 note, p. 50.
so, adv. or conj., *so**, thus,*
 correlative to als, da, *when,
 so much,* XI. 15 ; *such,*
 IX. 93.
Sohn, =es, "=e, m., *son**.
solch, adj., *such**.
sollen, *shall,* IX. 124 ; used
 absol., *to mean,* X. 9.
sonder, adj. for sonderbar,
 strange, IX. 46.
Sonne, =n, f., *sun.*
sonnen-hell, adj., lit. *sunbright,
 fair.*
Sonnen-schein, =(e)s, m., *sun-
 shine.*
spannen, *to stretch ; to bend ;
 to pitch,* XII. 54.

ſpát, adj. or adv., *late.*
Speer, =es, =e, m., *spear*.*
Speiſ(e), =n, f., *food.*
ſpicken, *to lard.*
ſpielen, *to play.*
Spieß, =es, =e, m., *dart, lance,* VIII. 22 [akin to — spit].
Splitter, =s, =, m., *splinter*, shiver.*
Sporn, =es, pl. Sporen, m., *spurs.*
Spott, =es, m., *scoffing, mockery.*
ſpöttlich, unusual form for ſpöttiſch [fr. ſpott], *scornfully, disdainfully.*
ſprach(en), pret. of ſprechen, *to speak*.*
ſprang, pret. of ſpringen, *to spring*; to jump.*
ſprechen (ſprach, geſprochen, ſprich), *to speak*; to say.*
ſprengen, *to gallop,* III. 7 [causative form of ſpringen, to spring; thus ſenken fr. ſinken, wenden fr. winden]; see p. 31.
ſpricht, pres. ind. of ſprechen, *to speak; to say.*
ſpringen (ſprang, geſprungen), *to spring*; to leap; to jump; to burst,* XIII. 36.

Spruch, =es, "=e, m., lit. *saying, command.*
Stab, =es, "=e, m., *staff.*
ſtach, pret. of ſtechen, *to sting; to pierce; to stab.*
Stadt, "=e, f., *town.*
Stahl, =s, "=, m., *steel*.*
Stahl=gewand, =es, "=er, n., lit. steel garment, *coat of mail.*
Stamm, =es, "=e, m., lit. stem*, stock, *race, family.*
Stand=halten (hielt ... Stand, Stand ... gehalten), *to be proof; to resist; to make head against.*
Stange, =n, f., *rod, pole, perch, lance,* X. 78.
ſtark, adj. or adv., *strong,* VIII. 12 ; *mighty* [akin to — stark].
Stätt(e), =n, f., *spot, place.*
ſtatt daß, conj., *instead* of.*
ſtattlich, adj. or adv., *stately, lordly,* XII. 20.
Staub, =es, m., *dust.*
ſtaunend, pres. part. of ſtaunen, used adv. *astonished, wondering.*
ſtechen (ſtach, geſtochen, ſtich), *to prick; to pierce; to thrust; to stab.*
ſtecken, lit. *to stick; to plant,* XII. 53.

ſtehen (ſtand, geſtanden), *to stand*.
ſteigen (ſtieg, geſtiegen), *to mount ; to ascend.*
Stein, =es, =e, m., *stone*, rock,* VII. 7.
ſteinern, adj., *stony*.*
Stein=wand, "=e, f., *stone* wall.*
Steuer, =s, =, n., *rudder, helm,* [akin to — steer] ; (die Steuer, tax, rate, etc.)
ſteuern, *to steer*.*
ſtieg(en) . . . auf, pret. of auf= ſteigen, *to mount.*
ſtieß, pret. of ſtoßen, *to push ; to blow,* I. 10.
ſtill, adj. or adv., *still* (adj.), *quiet.*
Stimme, =n, f., *voice.*
Stöhnen, =s, n., *groaning, moans.*
ſtolz, adj. or adv., *proud,* V. 1 [akin to — stilt, and to — stout].
Stolz, =es, m., *pride.*
Stoß, =es, "=e, m., *thrust, blow, shock,* XII. 42.
ſtoßen (ſtieß, geſtoßen), to push ; ins Horn —, *to blow the horn;* see note, p. 30.
Strahl, =es, =en, m., *ray.*
ſtrahlen, *to beam ; to stream,* XIII. 15 ; *to shine,* VII. 3.

Strand, =es, =e, m., *strand, seashore, beach.*
Streich, =es, =e, m., *stroke*, blow,* VIII. 31 ; *freak, prank,* 56.
ſtreichen (ſtrich, geſtrichen), *to stroke*.*
ſtreifen, *to roam ; to scour.*
Streit, =es, =e, m., *fight, combat.*
ſtritte, pret. subj. of ſtreiten, *to fight.*
Strom, =es, "=e, m., *stream, torrent.*
Stück, =es, =e, n., *piece, fragment,* V. 20 ; *bit, distance,* VIII. 17.
ſtumm, adj. or adv., *dumb, mute, silently,* IX. 44.
Stumpf, =es, "=e, m., *stump*.*
ſtund, obsol. pret. of ſtehen, *to stand.*
Sturm, =es, "=e, m., *storm* ;* im — e ſchreiten, *to make an assault* (Sturmſchritt, double quick pace).
ſtürmen, *to storm* ; to rage ;* see einſtürmen.
Sturmglock(e), =n, f., lit. *storm-bell, tocsin,* VII. 21.
ſtürzen, intrans. *to fall ; to tumble down.*
ſtutzen, intrans. *to stop short,* III. 8 ; *to be startled ;* trans., *to trim ; to crop.*

ſuchen, *to seek; to search; to look for.*

Süd, =ens, or Süden, =s, m., *south.*

ſüß, adj. or adv., *sweet*;* fig. *beloved,* IX. 9.

Süße, das, lit. *sweetness; tender affections.*

T

Tafel, =n, f., *table*;* cp. note, p. 36.

Tag, =es, =e, m., *day*.*

Tann, =es, m., = Tannenwald, *pine-wood.*

Tannenbaum, =es, "=e, m., comp. of Tanne, f. (fir) + baum (tree), i.e. *fir-tree.*

Tanz, =es, "=e, m., *dance*.*

tapfer, adj. or adv., *doughty, valiant* [akin to—dapper].

Tartſche, =n, f., *shield, buckler* [akin to—target; see note, p. 73].

teuer, adj. or adv., *dear*, scarce,* XI. 32.

Teufel, =s, =, m., *devil*.*

Thal, =es, "=er, n., *valley, dale*.*

that, pret. of thun, *did, uttered,* XI. 29.

thät, obsol. pret. of thun; see note, p. 34.

Thor, =es, =e, n., *gate, door*.*

Thron, =es, =e, m., *throne*.*

Thür(e), =n, f., *door*.*

Tiefe, =, =n, f. [fr. adj. tief, *deep*], *dale* [akin to — *depth*].

Tier, =es, =e, n., *animal, beast* [akin to—deer].

Tiſch, =es, =e, m., *table,* board [like Engl. dish, fr. Lat. discus].

Toben, n., infinit. used as subst., *raging.*

Tochter, "=, f., *daughter*.*

Töchterlein, n., dimin. of Tochter, *little daughter*.*

todt, adj. or adv., *dead*;* der Todte, =n, =n, m., *the dead one.*

Ton, =es, "=e, m., *tone*, voice.*

tönen, *to ring.*

tragen (trug, getragen), *to bear, to carry* [akin to—to draw; to drag].

trägt, third pers. sing., pres. indic. of tragen.

Trank, =es, "=e, m. [fr. pret. sing. of trinken], *drink*,* IX. 18.

trara, interj., *tally ho!*

trauen, *to trust;* reflexive—*to venture,* IX. 118 [akin to—true, and to—trow].

trauern, *to grieve; to mourn.*

träumen [fr. Traum], *to dream**; see note, p. 29.

traun! interj., *forsooth.*

traurig, adj. or adv., *sadly* [akin to—*dreary*].

treffen (traf, getroffen; trifft), *to hit*, VIII. 30.

treiben (trieb, getrieben), transit. *to drive;* reflex., *to separate; to part.*

treten (trat, getreten, tritt), *to tread; to step.*

treu, adj. or adv., *true*, faithful.*

Treue, f., *truth*, loyalty.*

trifft, third pers. sing., pres. indic. of treffen, *to hit.*

Trink=glas, =es, "=er, n., *drinking*-cup.*

trinken (trank, getrunken), *to drink*.*

tritt, third pers. sing., pres. indic. of treten, *to step.*

Tritt, =es, =e, m., *step, pace*, VI. 6 (fr. treten, to tread).

Trock(e)ne, n. subst. from adj. trocken, *dry land.*

Trommel, =n, f., *drum*.*

Trost, =es, m., *consolation, comfort*, IX. 16 [akin to—*trust*].

trotzig, adj. or adv., *proud, stubborn,* XII. 52; *defiant,* XIV. 30.

trüb(e), adj. or adv., *lit. troubled,* turbid; *gloomy, sad,* X. 148.

Truchseß, =es, =e, m., *lord high steward.*

trug, pret. of tragen, *to bear; to carry*, V. 7.

Trümmer=fall, =es, m., *ruins;* see note, p. 46.

Trunk, =es, "=, m. [fr. old pret. plur. of trinken, *i.e.* trunken], *drink**, VIII. 8.

trunken, adj. or adv., *drunken, drunk.*

Tuch, =es, "=er, n., *cloth.*

Türke, =n, =n, m., *Turk*.*

türkisch, adj., *Turkish*.*

Turm, =es, "=e, m., *tower*, turret.*

U

über, prep. gov. acc. or dat., *over*.*

überall, adv., *everywhere.*

über'm, contract. of über dem, *over the*.*

übermannen, *to overpower.*

über Nacht, lit. *over* (i.e. *during the*) *night*.*

überschallen, lit. *to surpass in sound; to drown*, VII. 14.

um, conj., *in order to.*

um, prep. gov. acc., *around, about*, XI. 15.
um, *for the sake of*, IX. 7, 123; X. 208.
umher, adv., *all round*.
um=kehren, ſich, *to turn round*.
umſonſt, adv., *in vain*.
unbehenbe, adj. or adv., *awkward, clumsy;* see note, p. 40.
ungefüg, adj., *uncouth*.
ungern, adv., reluctantly, *with sorrow*.
uns, pers. pr. acc. or dat. of wir, *us**.
unter, prep. gov. acc. or dat., *under*, beneath, below*.
Unterlaß, =es, m., *intermission, ceasing* [fr. unterlaſſen].
unterm, contract. of unter bem, *under the**.

V

Vaſall, =en, =en, m., *vassal**.
Vater, =s, "=, m., *father**, V. 2.
verbrannt, p.p. of verbrennen, *charred*.
verborren, *to wither*.
vereint, p.p. of vereinen, *to unite, together*, X. 30.
verführen, *to mislead; to decoy*.
vergelten (vergalt, vergolten), *to requite*, IX. 127.

vergeſſen (vergaß, vergeſſen), *to forget**.
vergönnen, *to allow; to grant*.
verhauchen, *to exhale; to breathe out*.
verlaſſen (verließ, verlaſſen), *to leave*.
verlernen, lit. *to unlearn*; to forbear from*.
verlieh(en), p.p. of verleihen, *to endow with*.
verlocken, *to seduce; to suborn*.
vermeinen, *to think; to suppose*.
vernimmt, third p. sing., pres. ind. of vernehmen, *to hear*.
vernommen, p.p. of vernehmen, *to hear*.
veröbet, p.p. of veröben, *waste, desolate*.
verröcheln, *to breathe one's last;* see note, p. 48.
verrucht, adj., *infamous*.
verſchlafen (verſchlief, verſchlaf=en), *to oversleep; to sleep away;* see note, p. 41.
verſchlang, pret. of verſchlingen, lit. *to engulf*.
verſchlingen (verſchlang, verſchlungen), *to engulf*, IX. 10.
verſchwunden, p.p. of verſchwin=ben, *to vanish*.
verſenken, *to sink**, transit., III. 3 [causative form of ſinken].

versiegen, to dry up.
versinken (versank, versunken), to sink down; to sink in oblivion, XIV. 64.
verspotten, to jeer at; to deride.
versteint, p.p. of versteine(r)n, lit. petrified, i.e. a heap of stones.
verstohlen, adj. or adv., stealthily.
verstoßen (verstieß, verstoßen), to toss about.
verstreuen, lit. to disperse; to spread, XIV. 62.
versuchen, to try; to tempt; to test.
versunken, p.p. of versinken, to sink down; sunk in oblivion; unremembered, XIV. 64.
verzich(e)n, with dat. of person, p.p. of verzeih(e)n, to forgive.
viel, much; pl. viele, many.
vier=fältig, adj. or adv., four-fold*.
vierfarb, adj. or adv., for vierfarbig, lit. four-coloured, i.e. motley.
viert(e), ord. numb., fourth*.
Viertel, =s, =, n., lit. quarter, ward, IX. 86.
Vögelein, =s, =, n., dim. of Vogel, little bird [akin to—fowl].

voll, adj. or adv., full*.
Voll=mond, =es, m., full moon*.
vom, contract. of von dem, from the.
von, prep. gov. dat., of, from.
vor, prep. gov. acc. or dat., before*; Schritt vor Schritt, VIII. 24; by.
vorbei (comp. of vor + bei), along by, i.e. passing by before some one.
Vorder=fuß, =e, "=e, m., fore-foot*.
vor=strömen, to stream forth.
vorüber=reiten (ritt ... vorüber, vorüber=geritten), to ride* by.

W

wachen, to watch; to be awake; to be on the alert, X. 55.
Wächter, =s, =, m., watchman, guard, warder, XV. 21.
Waffe, =n, f., or (X. 58) obsol.; das Waffen, weapon*, arms.
Waffen=stück, =es, n., piece of arms.
wafer, adj. or adv., brave, gallant [from wach, akin to —wake, i.e. alert].
Wald, =es, "=er, m., wood*, forest.
Wald=strom, =es, "=e, m., torrent.
Wall, =es, "=e, m., wall*.

wallen, *to flare*, VII. 27 ; *to boil*, VIII. 29 ; *to wave*, XII. 42.

wallen (poetical), to walk, to travel, especially to go on a pilgrimage ; hence Wall=fahrer, pilgrim ; Wallfahrt, pilgrimage.

wandern, *to wander* ; to rove*.

war, pret of sein, *was**.

wär(e), first or third pers. sing., pret. subj. of sein, *to be*.

ward, pret. of werden, IX. 26.

warm, adj. or adv., *warm*, warmly*.

warum, adv., *why*.

was, interrog. or relat. pron., absolutely—*what** ; adj., *what kind of*, VIII. 48.

was, for warum, *why*, XV. 1.

was für ein, *what kind (sort) of?*

waschen (wusch, gewaschen), *to wash**.

Wasser, =s, =, n., *water**.

Wat, f. ; see note, p. 37.

wecken, *to awaken**.

Weg, =es, =e, m., *way** ; seines Weges, adv., gen. of manner.

weg=geraubt, p.p. of weg=rauben, *to rob; to carry off ; to abduct*.

weg=gerissen, pret. of weg=reißen, lit. *to tear away ; to carry off*, VI. 8.

weg=reißen (riß . . . weg, weg=gerissen), *to tear away ; to carry off*, VI. 8.

Wegs, des, *along the way*, VIII. 45.

weh, interj., *woe*.

Wehmut, f., *sadness* (most compounds of Mut are fem., though Mut is masc.)

Wehr(e), =n, f., collective noun, *weapons*.

Weib, =es, =er, n., *woman, wife**, XIV. 33.

weich, adj. or adv., *soft, tender* [akin to—weak].

weil, conj., *because*.

Weil(e), f., *while**.

weilen, *to stay ; to tarry*, VII. 4 [akin to—while].

Wein, =es, =e, m., *wine**.

weiß, adj. or adv., *white**.

weit, adj. or adv., *wide, broad, far and wide*, V. 19.

Weite, =n, f., *distance ;* in die —, *far*.

weiter, adv., *further (on)*.

weiter=führen, *to lead on*.

Welle, =n, f., *wave, billow**.

Welt, =en, f., *world ;* see note, p. 34 [O. G. weralt, akin to—world].

VOCABULARY.

wenig, adv., *little;* wenige, *few.*
wer, absol. pron., *whoever,* IX. 19 ; interr. pr., *who?*
werden (wurde [ward], geworden), *to become,* aux. verb used to form pass. voice.
werfen (warf, geworfen, wirf), *to throw,* VIII. 22 [akin to—warp].
wert, adj. or adv., *worthy*.*
Wicht, =es, =e, m., *imp,* IX. 53 ; see note, p. 36 ; *wretch,* X. 209 [akin to—wight].
wie, adv. or adv. conj., *as, as soon as,* X. 93 ; *how,* V. 16.
wieder, adv., *again.*
Wieder=hall, =es, =e, m., *echo, re-echo.*
wieder=tönen, *to resound; to re-echo.*
wild, adj. or adv., *wild*, wildly, fiercely,* III. 10 ; IX. 116.
Wild=bret, =s, n., *game;* see note, p. 37.
Wilde, f., for die Wildnis, *wilderness*.*
Wilhelm, =s, *William*.*
Will=kommen, n., *welcome*.*
Wind, =es, =e, m., *wind*.*
Wink, =es, =e, m., *sign, beckoning* [akin to—wink].
winzig, adj., *little, tiny*.*

Wipfel, =s, =, m., *top, crown* (of a tree).
Wirt, =es, =e, m., *host, landlord, innkeeper.*
wog, pret. of wiegen, *to weigh,* IV. 3.
wohl, adv., *well, indeed,* I. 1 ; *probably,* IX. 90 ; *fain,* XI. 35 ; adv., *I wonder!* X. 143.
wohlauf! interj., *up! come on! well then!*
wohlgemut, adv., *cheerfully.*
wollen, irr. aux. v. of mood, *will*; to want; to be willing; to be about.*
wonnig, adj., *blissful.*
Wort, =es, pl. "=er, or Worte, n., *word*.*
Wuchs, =es, "=e, m. [fr. wuchs, pret. of wachsen], *growth, stature.*
wunderbar, adj. or adv., *wonderful*.*
wunder=klar, adj., *wonderfully bright.*
wundermild; see note, p. 30.
Wunderschild, =es, =e, m., *magic shield.*
wünschen, *to wish*.*
würd(e), third p. sing., pret. subj. of werden, aux. verb to form pass. voice, VIII. 43.

Wurzel, =n, f., *root* [akin to —wort; cp. also mangel wurzel].
wuſch, pret. of waſchen, *to wash**.
wüſt, adj. or adv., *waste*, *desert*, VIII. 4.
Wut, f., *fury, rage* [akin to —wrath*].
wüten, *to rage; to rave.*

Z

Zaum, =es, ″=e, m., *rein, bridle*, VIII. 14 [akin to—team].
zeigen, *to show.*
Zeit, =en, f., *time* [akin to—tide].
zerbrechlich, adj. or adv., *fragile, brittle**.
zerfloſſen, p.p. of zerfließen, *melted.*
zerhau(e)n, p.p. of zerhauen *to cut* (hew*) *up*, X. 136; *to chop*; see note, p. 36.
zerſchellen, *to dash to pieces.*
zerſprungen, p.p. of zerſpringen, *to burst.*
zerſtoben, p.p. of zerſtieben, *scattered as dust*; see note, p. 46.
zerſtört, p.p. of zerſtören, *to destroy.*
zertritt, third pers. sing., pres. indic. of zertreten, *to crush; to trample down.*
zeugen, *to bear witness*, XIV. 59.
zieh(e)n (zog, gezogen), *to draw; to drag*, X. 69 [akin to— to tug].
ziemen, with dat. of pers., *to suit; to be fitting for* [akin to—beseem].
Zierat, =es, =e, =(en), m., *ornament, trinket.*
Zins, =es, =e, m., *tribute;* see note, p 37.
zittern, *to tremble.*
zog, pret. of ziehen, *to pull; to drag;* zog nach, *wandered*, XIV. 9.
zögern, *to tarry; to hesitate*, XIII. 8.
zu, adv., *too**, IV. 4.
zu, prep. gov. dat., *to**, *at*, X. 141.
zu=decken, *to cover.*
Zug, =es, ″=e, m. [fr. pret. of ziehen, i.e. zog], *draught.*
zugehauen, p.p. of zu=hauen, *to rough hew**; *to dress.*
zugleich, adv., *at the same time.*
zuletzt, adv., *at last**; *last of all.*
zum, contract. of zu dem, *to the**.

VOCABULARY.

zürnen, with dat., to be angry, wroth.

zurück, adv. (comp. of zu, to, + Rück(en), back), backwards, III. 8.

zurück=bleiben (blieb ... zurück, zurück=geblieben), to fall behind; to lag; to be straggling, VIII. 18.

zurück=bringen, to bring back*.

zurück=springen (sprang ... zurück, zurück = gesprungen), to recoil, X. 84.

zu=rufen, with dat. (rief ... zu, zu=gerufen), to acclaim; to shout; to call out, VII. 18.

zusammen=gestückt, lit. together patched, i.e. patched up, IX. 38.

zusammen=nehmen, lit. to take together; to collect; to summon.

zusammt, prep. gov. dat. together with.

zwar, adv. (comp. of zu + wahr), indeed.

zweite, ord. numb., second.

zwier, obsol. for zweifach, twice*.

zwingen (zwang, gezwungen), to force.

zwölf, twelve*.

THE END.